TOUCHSTONE

MICHAEL MCCARTHY
JEANNE MCCARTEN
HELEN SANDIFORD

4

STUDENT'S BOOK

CAMBRIDGE
UNIVERSITY PRESS

CAMBRIDGE UNIVERSITY PRESS
Cambridge, New York, Melbourne, Madrid, Cape Town,
Singapore, São Paulo, Delhi, Mexico City

Cambridge University Press
32 Avenue of the Americas, New York, NY 10013–2473, USA

www.cambridge.org
Information on this title: www.cambridge.org/9780521665933

First published 2006
20th printing 2013

Printed in Hong Kong, China, by Golden Cup Printing Company Limited

A catalog record for this publication is available from the British Library.

ISBN 978-0-521-66593-3 pack consisting of student's book and self-study audio CD/CD-ROM (Windows®, Mac®)
ISBN 978-0-521-60144-3 pack consisting of student's book/Korea and self-study audio CD/CD-ROM (Windows®, Mac®)
ISBN 978-0-521-60145-0 pack consisting of student's book A and self-study audio CD/CD-ROM (Windows®, Mac®)
ISBN 978-0-521-60146-7 pack consisting of student's book B and self-study audio CD/CD-ROM (Windows®, Mac®)
ISBN 978-0-521-66592-6 workbook
ISBN 978-0-521-60147-4 workbook A
ISBN 978-0-521-60148-1 workbook B
ISBN 978-0-521-66591-9 teacher's edition
ISBN 978-0-521-66588-9 CDs (audio)
ISBN 978-0-521-66589-6 cassettes

Art direction, book design, photo research, and layout services: Adventure House, NYC
Audio production: Full House, NYC

Authors' acknowledgments

Touchstone has benefited from extensive development research. The authors and publishers would like to extend their particular thanks to the following reviewers, consultants, and piloters for their valuable insights and suggestions.

Reviewers and consultants:

Thomas Job Lane and Marilia de M. Zanella from **Associação Alumni**, São Paulo, Brazil; Simon Banha from **Phil Young's English School**, Curitiba, Brazil; Katy Cox from **Casa Thomas Jefferson**, Brasilia, Brazil; Rodrigo Santana from **CCBEU**, Goiânia, Brazil; Cristina Asperti, Nancy H. Lake, and Airton Pretini Junior from **CEL LEP**, São Paulo, Brazil; Sonia Cury from **Centro Britânico**, São Paulo, Brazil; Daniela Alves Meyer from **IBEU**, Rio de Janeiro, Brazil; Ayeska Farias from **Mai English**, Belo Horizonte, Brazil; Solange Cassiolato from **LTC**, São Paulo, Brazil; Fernando Prestes Maia from **Polidiomas**, São Paulo, Brazil; Chris Ritchie and Debora Schisler from **Seven Idiomas**, São Paulo, Brazil; Maria Teresa Maiztegui and Joacyr de Oliveira from **União Cultural EEUU**, São Paulo, Brazil; Sakae Onoda from **Chiba University of Commerce**, Ichikawa, Japan; James Boyd and Ann Conlon from **ECC Foreign Language Institute**, Osaka, Japan; Catherine Chamier from **ELEC**, Tokyo, Japan; Janaka Williams, Japan; David Aline from **Kanagawa University**, Yokohama, Japan; Brian Long from **Kyoto University of Foreign Studies**, Kyoto, Japan; Alistair Home and Brian Quinn from **Kyushu University**, Fukuoka, Japan; Rafael Dovale from **Matsushita Electric Industrial Co., Ltd.**, Osaka, Japan; Bill Acton, Michael Herriman, Bruce Monk, and Alan Thomson from **Nagoya University of Commerce**, Nisshin, Japan; Alan Bessette from **Poole Gakuin University**, Osaka, Japan; Brian Collins from **Sundai Foreign Language Institute, Tokyo College of Music**, Tokyo, Japan; Todd Odgers from **The Tokyo Center for Language and Culture**, Tokyo, Japan; Jion Hanagata from **Tokyo Foreign Language College**, Tokyo, Japan; Peter Collins and Charlene Mills from **Tokai University**, Hiratsuka, Japan; David Stewart from **Tokyo Institute of Technology**, Tokyo, Japan; Alberto Peto Villalobos from **Cenlex Santo Tomás**, Mexico City, Mexico; Diana Jones and Carlos Lizarraga from **Instituto Angloamericano**, Mexico City, Mexico; Raúl Mar and María Teresa Monroy from **Universidad de Cuautitlán Izcalli**, Mexico City, Mexico; JoAnn Miller from **Universidad del Valle de México**, Mexico City, Mexico; Orlando Carranza from **ICPNA**, Peru; Sister Melanie Bair and Jihyeon Jeon from **The Catholic University of Korea**, Seoul, South Korea; Peter E. Nelson from **Chung-Ang University**, Seoul, South Korea; Joseph Schouweiler from **Dongguk University**, Seoul, South Korea; Michael Brazil and Sean Witty from **Gwangwoon University**, Seoul, South Korea; Kelly Martin and Larry Michienzi from **Hankook FLS University**, Seoul, South Korea; Scott Duerstock and Jane Miller from **Konkuk University**, Seoul, South Korea; Athena Pichay from **Korea University**, Seoul, South Korea; Lane Darnell Bahl, Susan Caesar, and Aaron Hughes from **Korea University**, Seoul, South Korea; Farzana Hyland and Stephen van Vlack from **Sookmyung Women's University**, Seoul, South Korea; Hae-Young Kim, Terry Nelson, and Ron Schafrick from **Sungkyunkwan University**, Seoul, South Korea; Mary Chen and Michelle S. M. Fan from **Chinese Cultural University**, Taipei, Taiwan; Joseph Sorell from **Christ's College**, Taipei, Taiwan; Dan Aldridge and Brian Kleinsmith from **ELSI**, Taipei, Taiwan; Ching-Shyang Anna Chien and Duen-Yeh Charles Chang from **Hsin Wu Institute of Technology**, Taipei, Taiwan; Timothy Hogan, Andrew Rooney, and Dawn Young from **Language Training and Testing Center**, Taipei, Taiwan; Jen Mei Hsu and Yu-hwei Eunice Shih from **National Taiwan Normal University**, Taipei, Taiwan; Roma Starczewska and Su-Wei Wang from **PQ3R Taipei Language and Computer Center**, Taipei, Taiwan; Elaine Paris from **Shih Chien University**, Taipei, Taiwan; Jennifer Castello from **Cañada College**, Redwood City, California, USA; Dennis Johnson, Gregory Keech, and Penny Larson from **City College of San Francisco – Institute for International Students**, San Francisco, California, USA; Ditra Henry from **College of Lake County**, Gray's Lake, Illinois, USA; Madeleine Murphy from **College of San Mateo**, San Mateo, California, USA; Ben Yoder from **Harper College**, Palatine, Illinois, USA; Christine Aguila, John Lanier, Armando Mata, and Ellen Sellergren from **Lakeview Learning Center**, Chicago, Illinois, USA; Ellen Gomez from **Laney College**, Oakland, California, USA; Brian White from **Northeastern Illinois University**, Chicago, Illinois, USA; Randi Reppen from **Northern Arizona University**, Flagstaff, Arizona, USA; Janine Gluud from **San Francisco State University – College of Extended Learning**, San Francisco, California, USA; Peg Sarosy from **San Francisco State University – American Language Institute**, San Francisco, California, USA; David Mitchell from **UC Berkley Extension, ELP – English Language Program**, San Francisco, California, USA; Eileen Censotti, Kim Knutson, Dave Onufrock, Marnie Ramker, and Jerry Stanfield from **University of Illinois at Chicago – Tutorium in Intensive English**, Chicago, Illinois, USA; Johnnie Johnson Hafernik from **University of San Francisco, ESL Program**, San Francisco, California, USA; Judy Friedman from **New York Institute of Technology**, New York, New York, USA; Sheila Hackner from **St. John's University**, New York, New York, USA; Joan Lesikin from **William Paterson University**, Wayne, New Jersey, USA; Linda Pelc from **LaGuardia Community College**, Long Island City, New York, USA; Tamara Plotnick from **Pace University**, New York, USA; Lenore Rosenbluth from **Montclair State University**, Montclair, New Jersey, USA; Suzanne Seidel from **Nassau Community College**, Garden City, New York, USA; Debbie Un from **New York University, New School**, and **LaGuardia Community College**, New York, New York, USA; Cynthia Wiseman from **Hunter College**, New York, New York, USA; Aaron Lawson from **Cornell University**, Ithaca, New York, USA, for his help in corpus research; Belkis Yanes from **CTC Belo Monte**, Caracas, Venezuela; Victoria García from **English World**, Caracas, Venezuela; Kevin Bandy from **LT Language Teaching Services**, Caracas, Venezuela; Ivonne Quintero from **PDVSA**, Caracas, Venezuela.

Piloters:

Daniela Jorge from **ELFE Idiomas**, São Paulo, Brazil; Eloisa Marchesi Oliveira from **ETE Professor Camargo Aranha**, São Paulo, Brazil; Marilena Wanderley Pessoa from **IBEU**, Rio de Janeiro, Brazil; Marcia Lotaif from **LTC**, São Paulo, Brazil; Mirlei Valenzi from **USP English on Campus**, São Paulo, Brazil; Jelena Johanovic from **YEP International**, São Paulo, Brazil; James Steinman from **Osaka International College for Women**, Moriguchi, Japan; Brad Visgatis from **Osaka International University for Women**, Moriguchi, Japan; William Figoni from **Osaka Institute of Technology**, Osaka, Japan; Terry O'Brien from **Otani Women's University**, Tondabayashi, Japan; Gregory Kennerly from **YMCA Language Center** piloted at **Hankyu SHS**, Osaka, Japan; Daniel Alejandro Ramos and Salvador Enríquez Castaneda from **Instituto Cultural Mexicano-Norteamericano de Jalisco**, Guadalajara, Mexico; Patricia Robinson and Melida Valdes from **Universidad de Guadalajara**, Guadalajara, Mexico.

We would also like to thank the people who arranged recordings: Debbie Berktold, Bobbie Gore, Bill Kohler, Aaron Lawson, Terri Massin, Traci Suiter, Bryan Swan, and the many people who agreed to be recorded.

The authors would like to thank the **editorial** and **production** team: Sue Aldcorn, Janet Battiste, Sylvia P. Bloch, David Bohlke, Karen Brock, Jeff Chen, Sarah A. Cole, Sylvia Dare, Karen Davy, Jane Evison, Jill Freshney, Deborah Goldblatt, Paul Heacock, Louisa Hellegers, Cindee Howard, Eliza Jensen, Lesley Koustaff, Heather McCarron, Lise R. Minovitz, Diana Nam, Kathy Niemczyk, Sandra Pike, Danielle Power, Bill Preston, Janet Raskin, Mary Sandre, Tamar Savir, Susannah Sodergren, Shelagh Speers, Kayo Taguchi, Mary Vaughn, Jennifer Wilkin, Dorothy E. Zemach, and all the design and production team at Adventure House.

And these Cambridge University Press **staff** and **advisors**: Yumiko Akeba, Jim Anderson, Kanako Aoki, Mary Louise Baez, Carlos Barbisan, Alexandre Canizares, Cruz Castro, Kathleen Corley, Kate Cory-Wright, Riitta da Costa, Peter Davison, Elizabeth Fuzikava, Steven Golden, Yuri Hara, Catherine Higham, Gareth Knight, João Madureira, Andy Martin, Alejandro Martínez, Nigel McQuitty, Carine Mitchell, Mark O'Neil, Rebecca Ou, Antonio Puente, Colin Reublinger, Andrew Robinson, Dan Schulte, Kumiko Sekioka, Catherine Shih, Howard Siegelman, Ivan Sorrentino, Ian Sutherland, Alcione Tavares, Koen Van Landeghem, Sergio Varela, and Ellen Zlotnick.

In addition, the authors would like to thank Colin Hayes and Jeremy Mynott for making the project possible in the first place. Most of all, very special thanks are due to Mary Vaughn for her dedication, support, and professionalism. Helen Sandiford would like to thank her family and especially her husband, Bryan Swan, for his support and love.

Welcome to Touchstone!

We created the **Touchstone** series with the help of the *Cambridge International Corpus* of North American English. The corpus is a large database of language from everyday conversations, radio and television broadcasts, and newspapers and books.

Using computer software, we analyze the corpus to find out how people actually use English. We use the corpus as a "touchstone" to make sure that each lesson teaches you authentic and useful language. The corpus helps us choose and explain the grammar, vocabulary, and conversation strategies you need to communicate successfully in English.

Touchstone makes learning English fun. It gives you many different opportunities to interact with your classmates. You can exchange personal information, take class surveys, role-play situations, play games, and discuss topics of personal interest. Using **Touchstone**, you can develop confidence in your ability to understand real-life English and to express yourself clearly and effectively in everyday situations.

We hope you enjoy using **Touchstone** and wish you every success with your English classes.

Michael McCarthy
Jeanne McCarten
Helen Sandiford

Unit features

Getting started *presents new grammar in natural contexts such as articles, surveys, interviews, conversations, and anecdotes.*

Figure it out *challenges you to notice how grammar works.*

Grammar *is presented in clear charts.*

In conversation *panels tell you about the grammar and vocabulary that are most frequent in spoken North American English.*

Talk about it *encourages you to discuss interesting questions with your classmates.*

Building vocabulary and grammar *combines new vocabulary and structures in one presentation, often to teach the grammar of a particular vocabulary set. In some units, vocabulary and grammar are presented separately.*

Word sort *helps you organize vocabulary and then use it to interact with your classmates.*

Grammar exercises *give you practice with new structures and opportunities to exchange personal information with your classmates.*

Speaking and listening *skills are often practiced together. You listen to a variety of conversations based on real-life language. Tasks include "listen and react" activities.*

Conversation strategy helps you "manage" conversations better. In this lesson, you learn how to check your understanding by asking questions in the form of statements. The strategies are based on examples from the corpus.

Strategy plus teaches important words and expressions for conversation management, such as using **so** to start or close a topic.

Speaking naturally helps you understand and use natural pronunciation and intonation.

Reading has interesting texts from newspapers, magazines, interviews, and the Internet. The activities help you develop reading skills.

Writing tasks include stories, interview questions, letters, short articles, and proposals.

Help notes give you information on things like punctuation, linking ideas, and organizing information.

Vocabulary notebook is a page of fun activities to help you organize and write down vocabulary.

Fun facts from the corpus tell you the most frequent words and expressions for different topics.

Word builder activities give you extra words and expressions to research and learn, allowing you to extend your vocabulary even more.

Free talk helps you engage in free conversation with your classmates.

On your own is a practical task to help you learn vocabulary outside of class.

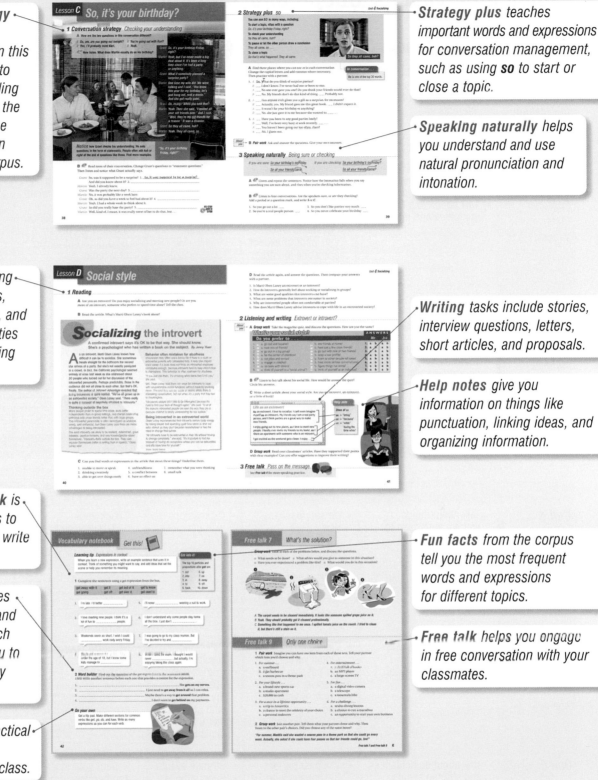

Other features

A **Touchstone checkpoint** after every three units reviews grammar, vocabulary, and conversation strategies.

A **Self-study Audio CD/ CD-ROM** gives you more practice with listening, speaking, and vocabulary building.

The **Class Audio Program** presents the conversations and listening activities in natural, lively English.

The **Workbook** gives you language practice and extra reading and writing activities. **Progress checks** help you assess your progress.

Touchstone Level 4 Scope and sequence

	Functions / Topics	Grammar	Vocabulary	Conversation strategies	Pronunciation
Unit 1 *Interesting lives* *pages 1–10*	▪ Ask questions to find out about someone's interests and background ▪ Tell interesting stories about your own life	▪ Review of simple and continuous forms of verbs ▪ Verbs followed by verb + -ing or to + verb	▪ Verbs followed by verb + -ing or to + verb	▪ Use the present tense to highlight key moments in a story ▪ Use this and these to highlight important people, things, and events in a story	▪ Reductions of auxiliary verbs and the pronoun you in questions
Unit 2 *Personal tastes* *pages 11–20*	▪ Talk about makeovers, style, and fashion ▪ Talk about your tastes in clothes and music	▪ Make comparisons with as . . . as and not as . . . as ▪ Ask negative questions when you want or expect someone to agree with you	▪ Colors, patterns, materials, and styles of clothing	▪ Show understanding by summarizing what people say ▪ Use Now to introduce a follow-up question on a different aspect of a topic	▪ Linking words with the same consonant sound
Unit 3 *World cultures* *pages 21–30*	▪ Talk about aspects of your culture ▪ Talk about manners, customs, and culturally appropriate behavior	▪ The simple present passive ▪ Verb + -ing as a subject and after prepositions ▪ to + verb after It's . . . ▪ Position of not	▪ Cultural items, icons, and events ▪ Manners, customs, and culturally appropriate behavior	▪ Use expressions like in fact to sound more direct when you speak ▪ Use of course to give information that is not surprising, or to show you understand or agree	▪ Silent syllables in which unstressed vowels are not pronounced

Touchstone checkpoint Units 1–3   pages 31–32

	Functions / Topics	Grammar	Vocabulary	Conversation strategies	Pronunciation
Unit 4 *Socializing* *pages 33–42*	▪ Talk about things you are supposed to do, things you were supposed to do, and things that are supposed to happen ▪ Talk about going out and socializing	▪ be supposed to, was / were supposed to, and was / were going to ▪ Inseparable phrasal verbs	▪ Expressions with get	▪ Check your understanding by using questions in the form of statements ▪ Use so to start or close a topic, to check your understanding, to pause, or to let someone draw a conclusion	▪ Intonation of sentences when you are sure vs. when you are checking
Unit 5 *Law and order* *pages 43–52*	▪ Talk about rules and regulations ▪ Talk about crime and punishment	▪ The passive of modal verbs ▪ get passive vs. be passive ▪ catch + verb + -ing	▪ Rules and regulations ▪ Crimes and offenses, the people who commit them, and punishments	▪ Organize your views with expressions like First (of all) ▪ Show someone has a valid argument with expressions like That's a good point	▪ Saying conversational expressions
Unit 6 *Strange events* *pages 53–62*	▪ Talk about coincidences and strange events ▪ Talk about belief in superstitions	▪ The past perfect ▪ Responses with So and Neither	▪ Strange events ▪ Superstitions from around the world	▪ Repeat your ideas in another way to make your meaning clear ▪ Use just to make your meaning stronger or softer	▪ Stressing new information

Touchstone checkpoint Units 4–6   pages 63–64

Listening	Reading	Writing	Vocabulary notebook	Free talk
A lucky escape ▪ Listen for details in a story, and retell it with a partner; then role-play a conversation about it *Facing a challenge* ▪ Listen to a true story, and answer questions	*My story: Pat Galloway* ▪ A magazine article about a successful engineer and the story of how she chose her profession	▪ Write a story about a time in your life when you faced a challenge ▪ Format for writing an anecdote or a story	*Mottoes* ▪ Write down the verb forms that can follow new verbs, and use them in sentences	*An interview with . . .* ▪ Pair work: Complete interesting questions to ask a classmate; then interview each other, and note your partner's answers
My music collection ▪ Listen for details in a conversation, and answer questions; then listen and choose the best responses *What's your thing?* ▪ Listen to four people talk about their tastes, and identify the topics they discuss; then listen and answer questions	*A free spirit!* ▪ An interview with a woman with very individual tastes	▪ Write questions to interview a partner on his or her personal style; write answers to your partner's questions ▪ Punctuation review: comma, dash, and exclamation mark	*Blue suede shoes* ▪ Find and label pictures that illustrate new words	*What's popular?* ▪ Group work: Discuss questions about current popular tastes and how tastes have changed
Away from home ▪ Listen to a woman talk about being away from home, and answer questions as she would *Favorite proverbs* ▪ Listen to four people talk about proverbs, and number them; then match them with English equivalents, and listen to check	*Counting Chickens* ▪ A magazine article about the use and misuse of proverbs	▪ Write an article about your favorite proverb and how it relates to your life ▪ Useful expressions for writing about proverbs or sayings	*Travel etiquette* ▪ Find examples of new words and expressions you have learned in magazines, in newspapers, and on the Internet	*Local customs* ▪ Pair work: Prepare a presentation on local customs for visitors to your country, and then present it to the class

Touchstone checkpoint Units 1–3   pages 31–32

Listening	Reading	Writing	Vocabulary notebook	Free talk
What are you like? ▪ Listen to people talk about plans, and summarize them; then listen and complete sentences as the man would *Extrovert or Introvert?* ▪ Take a quiz; then listen to a man talk about his social style, and answer the quiz as he would	*Socializing the introvert* ▪ A magazine article about a book on introverts living in an extroverted society	▪ Write an article about your own social style as an extrovert, an introvert, or a little of both ▪ Uses of *as*	*Get this!* ▪ Learn new expressions by writing example sentences that use them in context	*Pass on the message.* ▪ Class activity: Play a game where you pass a message to a classmate through another classmate, and then listen to see if your message is delivered correctly
We got robbed! ▪ Listen to a conversation, and answer questions; then listen and choose true sentences *Different points of view* ▪ Listen to a debate, and answer questions; then listen and respond to different points of view	*Cam phones, go home!* ▪ A magazine article about the cam-phone craze	▪ Write a letter to the editor of a magazine, responding to the article on cam phones ▪ Give reasons with *because*, *since*, and *as*	*It's a crime!* ▪ Write down new words in word charts that group related ideas together by topic	*Lawmakers* ▪ Pair work: Choose a topic and debate the pros and cons of three possible new laws; then join another pair with the same topic, and compare arguments
It's a small world! ▪ Listen to a woman tell a story, and answer questions *Lucky or not?* ▪ Listen to four people talk about superstitions, and determine if the things they are about are lucky or unlucky; then listen and write down each superstition	*Separated at birth . . .* ▪ A magazine article about the true story of twins who found each other after growing up in different adoptive families	▪ Write a true story from your own family history ▪ Prepositional time clauses	*Keep your fingers crossed.* ▪ Use word webs to group new sayings or superstitions by topic	*Can you believe it?* ▪ Pair work: Take turns telling each other true stories about unusual beliefs and strange events in your life

Touchstone checkpoint Units 4–6   pages 63–64

	Functions / Topics	Grammar	Vocabulary	Conversation strategies	Pronunciation
Unit 7 *Problem solving* pages 65–74	• Talk about errands and solving problems • Talk about things you do yourself and things you get done somewhere else • Talk about things that need to be fixed	• Causative *get* and *have* • *need* + passive infinitive • *need* + verb + *-ing*	• Errands • Household problems	• Speak informally in "shorter sentences" • Use expressions like *Oops!* and *Uh-oh!* when something goes wrong	• Short question and statement intonation
Unit 8 *Behavior* pages 75–84	• Talk about your reactions and behavior in different situations • Describe other people's emotions and personal qualities • Talk about hypothetical situations in the past	• Use *would have, should have,* and *could have* to talk hypothetically about the past • Use *must have, may have, might have,* and *could have* to speculate about the past	• Emotions and personal qualities • Expressions describing behavior	• Use expressions such as *That reminds me (of)* . . . to share experiences • Use *like* informally in conversation	• Reduction of *have* in past modals
Unit 9 *Material world* pages 85–94	• Talk about possessions and being materialistic • Discuss money and money management	• Reported speech • Reported questions	• Expressions to describe ownership and possessions • Money	• Report the content of conversations you have had • Quote other people or other sources of information	• Intonation of finished and unfinished ideas

Touchstone checkpoint Units 7–9   pages 95–96

	Functions / Topics	Grammar	Vocabulary	Conversation strategies	Pronunciation
Unit 10 *Fame* pages 97–106	• Discuss hypothetical situations in the past and what might (not) have happened to you and others if things had been different • Talk about celebrities and being famous	• Use *if* clauses with the past perfect form of the verb to talk hypothetically about the past • Tag questions	• Expressions to describe becoming famous, being famous, and losing fame	• Use tag questions to soften advice and give encouragement • Answer difficult questions with expressions like *It's hard to say*	• Intonation of tag questions
Unit 11 *Trends* pages 107–116	• Describe social and urban change • Describe environmental problems	• The passive of the present continuous and present perfect • Link ideas to express a contrast, reason, purpose, or alternative	• Expressions to describe change • Environmental problems	• Refer back to points made earlier in a conversation • Use more formal vague expressions like *and so forth* and *etc.*	• Reduction of auxiliary verbs
Unit 12 *Careers* pages 117–126	• Talk about planning a career • Discuss different jobs people do • Talk about hopes and expectations for the future	• *What* clauses and long noun phrases as subjects • The future continuous and future perfect	• Expressions to describe a job search • Areas of work, professions, and jobs	• Introduce what you say with expressions like *The best part was (that)* . . . • Use *I don't know if* . . . to introduce a statement and involve the other person in the topic	• Stressing *I* and *you*

Touchstone checkpoint Units 10–12   pages 127–128

Listening	Reading	Writing	Vocabulary notebook	Free talk
Wedding on a budget • Listen to a conversation, and check what the people agree on; then listen for what they'll do themselves or have done professionally *Fix it!* • Match four conversations with pictures; then listen to determine if the problems were solved	*Developing Your Problem-Solving Skills* • A magazine article about the importance of developing good problem-solving skills	• Write a proposal presenting a solution to a problem at school • Format for presenting a problem and its solution	*Damaged goods* • Find out if new words have different forms that can express the same idea, and use them in sentences	*What's the solution?* • Group work: Discuss the problems shown in four illustrations, and suggest possible solutions and advice
Similar experiences • Listen to two people share experiences, and number the incidents in order; then answer questions *Rude behavior* • Listen to a conversation, and number the items in a survey; then listen and write responses to opinions	*When and How to Apologize* • An article about the importance of apologizing and suggesting ways to do so	• Write a note of apology for something you did in the past • Expressions for writing a note of apology	*People watching* • Learn new vocabulary by making a connection with something or someone you know, and write true sentences	*Analyzing behavior* • Group work: Read about three situations, and discuss questions about people's behavior in each one
Who's materialistic? • Listen to someone answer questions, and take notes; then report his answers *I couldn't live without . . .* • Listen to four people talk about things they couldn't live without, and complete a chart; then listen and write responses to opinions	*Everything must go online!* • A magazine article about a man who sold all his belongings on the Internet	• Write an article about your classmates and things they feel they couldn't live without • Use of reporting verbs for direct speech and reported speech	*Get rich!* • When you learn a new word, notice its collocations – the words that are used with it	*Only one choice* • Pair work: Choose items from six sets, and explain your choices; then join another pair, and report your partner's choices

*Touchstone **checkpoint** Units 7–9   pages 95–96*

Listening	Reading	Writing	Vocabulary notebook	Free talk
Advice • Listen to a conversation, and answer questions about the details *Success is . . .* • Listen to four conversations about success, and complete sentences; then listen and complete a chart	*Renée: "I knew I'd pull through."* • A magazine article about actress Renée Zellweger and the challenges she faced while becoming successful	• Write a paragraph about someone you know who has achieved success, and explain why that person became successful • Topic and supporting sentences in a paragraph	*Do your best!* • Learn new idioms by writing example sentences that explain or clarify meaning	*Quotations* • Group work: Discuss six quotations about success by famous people; then make up your own definition of success to share with the class
Changes we see • Listen to four conversations about trends, and complete a chart; then listen to check if the people think the trends are good and why *Changing your life* • Listen to three people talk about technology, and match with photos; then listen and write why each one likes the technology	*Gadgets we love!* • An interview with two people about their use of new technology	• Write an article about a new technology you use and how it has changed your life • Expressions for describing trends	*Try to explain it!* • Write definitions in your own words to help you learn the meaning of new words and expressions	*Save the world!* • Group work: Create a campaign to improve the world in some way, and then present it to the class
What's she doing now? • Listen to a woman talk about her job, and answer questions; then listen to check details *A fabulous opportunity!* • Fill in the blanks in a job ad, and listen to a conversation about it to check guesses; then listen and answer questions	*Perfect answers to tough and tricky interview questions* • A magazine article about how to answer the most common questions in job interviews	• Write a letter of application for a job in response to an ad • Format for writing a letter of application	*From accountant to zoologist* • When you learn a new word, learn other words with the same root as well as common collocations to expand your vocabulary quickly	*Job fair* • Group work: Choose a job ad, and prepare for an interview; then answer questions as your group interviews you for the job

*Touchstone **checkpoint** Units 10–12   pages 127–128*

Useful language for . . .

Working in groups

We're ready now, aren't we?

Are we ready? Let's get started.

Haven't I interviewed you already?

I've already interviewed you, haven't I?

Where are we?

We're on number _____ .

We haven't quite finished yet.

Neither have we.

We still need more time – just a few more minutes.

So do we.

One interesting thing we found out was that _____ .

_____ told us that _____ .

Checking with the teacher

Would it be OK if I missed our class tomorrow? I have to _____ .

I'm sorry I missed the last class. What do I need to do to catch up?

When are we supposed to hand in our homework?

Excuse me. My homework needs to be checked.

I'm sorry. I haven't finished my homework. I was going to do it last night, but _____ .

Will we be reviewing this before the next test?

"_____" means "_____," doesn't it? It's a regular verb, isn't it?

I'm not sure I understand what we're supposed to do. Could you explain the activity again, please?

Could I please be excused? I'll be right back.

Interesting lives

In Unit 1, you learn how to . . .

■ use simple and continuous forms of verbs (review).

■ use verbs that are followed by verb + *-ing* or *to* + verb.

■ tell an interesting story about your life.

■ use the present tense to highlight key moments in a story.

■ use *this* and *these* to highlight Important people, things, and events.

Before you begin . . .

Do you know any interesting people?

Why do you think they are interesting?

What interesting things do they do?

English Department Newsletter

Student of the month – Melida Cortez

You should really get to know **Melida Cortez**, a graduate student in our English Department. Also a talented artist, she spends her free time painting, and she started a sculpture class last month. She hopes one day to have an exhibition of her work.

How long have you been living here?
I've been living in Mexico City for five years. I came here to go to school originally. It's a great place to live.

Have you ever lived in another country?
No, I haven't. But my brother has. He's been living in Bogotá, in Colombia, for almost a year now. I'm going to visit him later this year.

What kind of music are you listening to currently?
Well, of course I love Latin music. I'm listening to a lot of Latin jazz right now. I like to listen to music when I paint.

What's your favorite way of spending an evening? What do you do?
I like to go out with my friends – we go and eat someplace, and then go dancing all night!

When did you last buy yourself a treat?
Last week, actually. I was at a friend's art studio, and I fell in love with one of her paintings. So I bought it.

What did you do for your last birthday?
I went home and had a big party with my family.

What's the nicest thing anyone has ever done for you?
Actually, about six months ago, I was complaining to my dad that I didn't know how to drive, so he paid for some driving lessons. I was thrilled.

Who or what is the greatest love of your life?
Oh, chocolate! I can't get through the day without some.

What were you doing at this time yesterday?
I was sitting on a bus. We were stuck in traffic for an hour!

1 Getting started

A Read the interview with Melida. Do you have anything in common with her? Tell the class.

Figure it out

B Can you choose the correct form of each question? Circle *a* or *b*. Use the interview above to help you. Then ask and answer the questions with a partner.

1. a. What book do you read currently?
   b. What book are you reading currently?
2. a. When did you last see a really good movie?
   b. When were you last seeing a really good movie?
3. a. Have you ever stayed up all night?
   b. Have you ever been staying up all night?

2 Grammar Simple and continuous verbs (review)

Simple verbs: for completed actions or permanent situations	**Continuous verbs: for ongoing actions or temporary situations**

What kind of music **do** you **listen** to?
    I **love** Latin music. I **listen** to it a lot.
	What kind of music **are** you **listening** to currently?
	    I'm **listening** to a lot of Latin jazz right now.

Have you ever **lived** in another country?
    No, I've never **lived** anywhere else.
	How long **have** you **been living** here?
	    I've **been living** here for five years.

What **did** you **do** for your last birthday?
    I **went** home and **had** a big party.
	What **were** you **doing** at this time yesterday?
	    I **was sitting** on a bus.

A Complete the questions and answers. Use the simple or continuous form of the verb in the present, past, or present perfect. Then practice with a partner.

1. *A* Who _do_ you ___admire___ (admire) the most?
   B I _____ (admire) my grandfather. He _____ (teach) me a lot when I _____ (grow up).

2. *A* _____ you ever _____ (meet) anyone famous?
   B No, but last year, I _____ (see) a TV star on the street. We _____ both _____ (wait) in line for ice cream.

3. *A* When _____ you last _____ (get) a good workout?
   B Yesterday. In fact, I _____ (lift) weights when you _____ (call) me last night.

4. *A* What _____ you _____ (do) for a living?
   B Actually, I _____ (not work) right now. I _____ (look) for a job for six months, but I _____ (not find) anything yet.

5. *A* What _____ you _____ (do) for fun lately?
   B Not much. I _____ (work) really hard for the past year. In fact, I _____ (not take) a vacation in over a year now.

➤ **B** *Pair work* Ask and answer the questions. Give your own answers.

3 Speaking naturally Reductions in questions

How long **have you** been learning English? What **do you** like to do in your English class?	Why **are you** learning English? What **did you** do in your last class?

A Listen and repeat the questions. Notice the reductions of the auxiliary verbs and the pronoun *you*. Then ask and answer the questions with a partner.

➤ **B** *Pair work* Take turns asking the questions in the interview on page 2. Pay attention to your pronunciation of the auxiliary verbs and the pronoun *you*.

1 *Building vocabulary and grammar*

A  Listen to Dan's story. Answer the questions.

1. Where did Dan live before he moved to Seoul?
2. Why did he want to go to South Korea?
3. How did he get his job there?
4. What did his new company offer him?

Living abroad:
Dan's story

Dan Anderson was born in the U.S.A. He's now living in South Korea. We asked him, "How did you **end up** living in Seoul?"

Dan: Well, it's a long story! Before I came here, I **spent** three years working for a small company in Tokyo while I **finished** doing my master's in business. To be honest, I wasn't **planning on** leaving or anything. But one day, I **happened** to be in the office, and one of the salesmen was reading the newspaper.

He knew I was **considering** going to South Korea someday – you see, my mother's Korean, and I've always been interested in the culture and everything – and anyway, he leaned over and said, "Dan, this **seems** to be the perfect job for you. Check this out."

I looked at the ad, and I **remember** thinking, "Should I **bother** to apply?" But I **decided** to go for it even though I didn't **expect** to get it, and to make a long story short, I got the job!

The company **offered** to transfer me to Seoul, and they **agreed** to pay for my Korean lessons. I **started** working here two months later. And the rest is history.

I mean, I **miss** living in Japan, but you can't have it both ways, I guess. Actually, I can't **imagine** living anywhere else now!

> Word
> sort

B Can you sort the verbs in bold above into the correct categories? Which verbs are followed by verb + *-ing*? Which are followed by *to* + verb?

Verbs followed by verb + *-ing*		Verbs followed by *to* + verb	
end up (living)		happen (to be)	
spend (3 years working)			

2 Grammar *Verb complements: verb + -ing or to + verb*

Verb + verb + -ing: consider finish imagine miss mind spend **(time)**	He **finished reading** his newspaper. I **spent** three years **working** in Tokyo.
Verb + particle/preposition + verb + -ing: end up keep on think about plan on	How did you **end up living** here? I wasn't **planning on leaving** Japan.
Verb + to + verb: agree decide happen offer seem intend expect	They **agreed to pay** for Korean lessons. I didn't **expect to get** the job.
Verb + -ing or to + verb with a different meaning: remember stop try	I **stopped talking** to him. I **stopped to talk** to him.
Verb + -ing or to + verb with the same meaning: begin bother continue start like love hate	Should I **bother applying**? Should I **bother to apply**?

Complete the conversations with the correct forms of the verbs given. Then practice with a partner.

> **In conversation . . .**
>
> **Begin**, **bother**, **continue**, **like**, **love**, and **hate** are followed more often by **to +** **verb**. **Start** is followed more often by **verb + -ing**.

1. *A* How did you end up <u>studying</u> (study) here?
   B My friend recommended this school, so I decided _____ (sign up) for this class. How about you?
   A Well, I wasn't planning on _____ (learn) English, but my company offered _____ (pay) for my classes. I agreed _____ (come), and here I am! I want to keep on _____ (take) classes if I can.

2. *A* How did you get your current job?
   B It's a long story! I started _____ (work) there as an assistant, and I spent months just _____ (file) papers. I didn't mind _____ (do) that for a while, but then I happened _____ (hear) about a new sales position. I never intended _____ (be) a sales rep, but now I can't imagine _____ (do) anything else.

3 Talk about it *How did you end up doing that?*

Group work Has anyone in your group done these things? Find out the whole story. Ask the follow-up questions below, and add more questions of your own.

Who . . .
► has taken an interesting class?
► used to have an unusual job?
► has met a celebrity?
► has taken an exotic trip?
► used to have a bad habit?
► has done something scary?

Then ask:
What made you decide to do that?
How did you end up working there?
Were you expecting to meet him or her?
Are you planning on going again?
What made you stop doing that?
Would you ever consider doing that again?

4 Vocabulary notebook *Mottoes*

See page 10 for a new way to log and learn vocabulary.

We're both getting scared. . . .

1 Conversation strategy *Highlighting key moments in a story*

A Juan is telling his friend Kim a story. Underline the verbs in his sentences below. What tenses does he use?

Juan We were on this trail, and it was getting dark. Then Bryan says, "Where are we?"

Now listen to Juan and Bryan tell Kim the whole story. What happened to them?

Juan	Remember that time we were hiking in Utah?
Bryan	When we got lost? That was funny.
Kim	Why? What happened?
Juan	We were on this trail, and it was getting dark. Then Bryan says, "Where are we?"
Bryan	Yeah, we couldn't see a thing, and we walked off the trail. It was that bad.
Juan	Yeah, there were all these trees around us, and we were so lost. And we're thinking, "Oh, no." And we're both getting kind of scared. We just wanted to get out of there.
Kim	I bet.
Juan	And Bryan says, "Should we jog a little?" And I go, "Yeah. I was thinking the same thing. Let's go."
Bryan	So we started jogging, . . .
Juan	And we said to each other, "We've got to stick together, in case anything happens."

Notice how Juan changes to the present tense at key moments in his story. It makes them more "dramatic." Find examples in the conversation.

"We're both getting kind of scared."

B Read more of their conversation. Change the underlined verbs to the simple present or present continuous to make the story more dramatic. Then listen and check your answers.

Bryan Yeah. And all of a sudden, we <u>heard</u> this noise.

Juan And I <u>looked</u> over at Bryan, and I <u>saw</u> his face <u>was</u> white, and he <u>was starting</u> to run fast.

Bryan Well, yeah. I mean, it was a weird noise.

Juan So, I <u>was thinking</u>, "Wait a minute. What happened to our plan to stick together?" So I <u>started</u> to run with him.

Bryan Yeah, we <u>were running</u> through the trees, scared to death. It was hilarious! It was just like in a movie.

SELF-STUDY
AUDIO CD
CD-ROM

2 Strategy plus *this and these in stories*

When you tell stories, you can use ***this*** and ***these*** to highlight important people, things, and events.

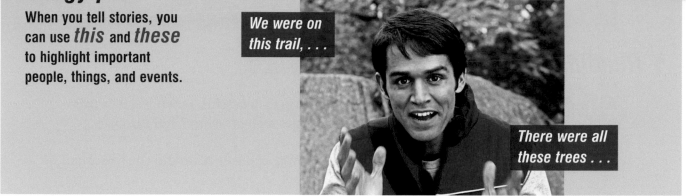

We were on this trail, . . .

There were all these trees . . .

A *Pair work* Replace *a*, *an*, and *some* with *this* or *these* in the stories below. Then take turns telling the stories.

1. "I have **an** aunt who's really into old paintings – she's always buying them at junk shops and yard sales. And in every room in her house, she has **some** old pictures on all the walls. Well, one time she goes to **a** yard sale, sees **a** picture, and buys it for practically nothing. And guess what? It turned out to be worth thousands!"

2. "I have **a** friend who's always getting into funny situations. One time she was invited to **a** party, and she got totally lost. Anyway, she sees **a** house with **some** cars parked in front of it, and she thought it was the right place. So she knocks on the door, and **a** nice guy lets her in. She had dinner there and everything before she realized it was the wrong party!"

About you → **B** *Pair work* Tell one of the stories above from memory, or tell an interesting story of your own. Remember to use *this* or *these* to highlight important people, things, and events.

3 Listening and speaking *A lucky escape*

A You're going to hear Aaron tell a story about a skiing accident. He was skiing with some friends when one of them fell down the mountain. Circle four questions you want to ask Aaron.

1. Where were you skiing?
2. How far did your friend fall?
3. What did you do when he fell?
4. How badly was he hurt?

5. Did you get help? How?
6. Did he have to go to the hospital?
7. When did this happen?
8. Is he OK now?

B Listen. Write answers to the questions you chose. Then share answers with a partner. Can you remember the story together? Consult other classmates if necessary.

C *Pair work* Role-play a conversation about the accident. Take turns telling the story and asking the questions.

Against the odds

1 Reading

A Think of someone you know who has become very successful. In what way is this person successful? Did he or she face any challenges along the way? Tell the class.

B Read the article. What profession did Pat Galloway choose? What did she like about it?

My story: Pat Galloway
"Bad idea. You'll flunk out."
A successful engineer tells her story.

When I was in high school in Kentucky in 1974, I was into the arts. I was a dancer, in the drama club, on the debate team. I was an artist. I had no chemistry, no physics, and no calculus at all. But one day at a required high school lecture, a civil-engineering professor from the University of Kentucky arrived to speak, showing all these renderings of buildings. I was fascinated with the fact that I might be able to draw and get paid for it. And according to him, I could improve the quality of life for people and be a problem solver. Well, I became so excited, I went home and told my mother, a teacher, that I wanted to be a civil engineer. My mother had a motto that I have followed to this day: "If you really want to do something, you put your mind to it. Don't ever let anyone tell you it can't be done." So when I told her, she said, "Great."

Then reality hit when I went back to my guidance counselor the next day and told him that instead of being a lawyer or an interior decorator, I now wanted to be an engineer. He looked at me and said, "Bad idea. You haven't scored on your aptitude test to be an engineer. You're not inclined to be an engineer. You're not made up to be an engineer." Then I went to my math teacher, and she said the same thing, "Bad idea. You'll flunk out."

I went to my grandmother, and her reaction was, "Isn't that a man's job?" And that's what really solidified it. I had two people tell me I wasn't intelligent enough, which I couldn't understand because I was a straight-A student, and now I had someone else tell me that it was a man's job. So I was bound and determined to prove everyone wrong. And I did. In 1978, I graduated from Purdue University in three years with a B+ average and a degree in civil engineering.

– as told to Deirdre van Dyk

C What do these words and expressions from the article mean? Choose *a* or *b*. How did you guess the meaning? Tell a partner.

1. you'll flunk out   a. you'll fail and leave college   b. you'll graduate
2. renderings   a. photographs   b. drawings
3. according to him   a. he said   b. I said
4. a motto   a. a promise   b. a rule to live by
5. put your mind to it   a. forget about it   b. try hard to do it
6. you're not inclined to be   a. you're not the type to be   b. you're not afraid to be
7. solidified it   a. convinced me   b. worried me
8. I was bound and determined   a. I was very angry   b. I was very focused

D Read the article again. Are the sentences true or false?
Correct the false sentences.

	True	False
1. Pat always planned on being a civil engineer.	☐	☐
2. She first became interested in engineering because she loved math and science.	☐	☐
3. Her mother encouraged her to follow her dream.	☐	☐
4. Pat's teachers expected her to be in a profession like engineering.	☐	☐
5. Pat wanted to prove to everyone that she could be a civil engineer.	☐	☐
6. Pat refused to let any problems stop her along the way.	☐	☐

2 Listening and writing *Facing a challenge*

A Listen to a true story about Lance Armstrong. Complete the sentences with the
correct information. Choose *a*, *b*, or *c*.

1. As a teenager, Lance Armstrong became a professional _____ .
   a. swimmer   b. cyclist   c. triathlete

2. He says he got his ambition from his _____ .
   a. close friend   b. mother   c. high school teacher

3. He is now _____ athlete.
   a. an amateur   b. a professional   c. a retired

4. The biggest challenge he faced was _____ .
   a. a serious illness   b. the media   c. losing races

5. He has won more _____ than anyone else.
   a. cycling races   b. Olympic medals   c. Tour de France races

B Think about a time in your life when you had to do something difficult. What did you
have to do? How did you feel? How did you feel afterwards? Write a story about that time.

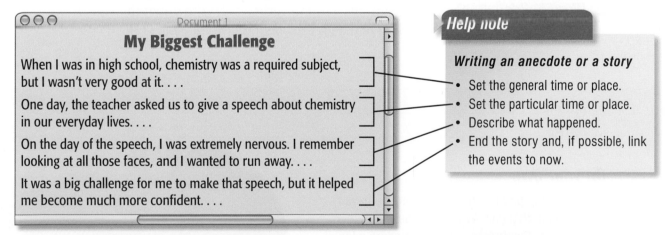

Document 1

My Biggest Challenge

When I was in high school, chemistry was a required subject,
but I wasn't very good at it. . . .

One day, the teacher asked us to give a speech about chemistry
in our everyday lives. . . .

On the day of the speech, I was extremely nervous. I remember
looking at all those faces, and I wanted to run away. . . .

It was a big challenge for me to make that speech, but it helped
me become much more confident. . . .

Help note

Writing an anecdote or a story

• Set the general time or place.
• Set the particular time or place.
• Describe what happened.
• End the story and, if possible, link
  the events to now.

C *Pair work* Read a partner's story. Then ask questions to find out more about the story.

3 Free talk *An interview with . . .*

See *Free talk 1* at the back of the book for more speaking practice.

Mottoes

Learning tip *Verb patterns*

When you learn a new verb, write down the verb form(s) that can follow it.
Then use it in a sentence. For example:

imagine verb + -ing	I can't imagine having lots of money.
decide to + verb	I've decided to be a doctor.
start verb + -ing	I'm going to start saving money.
start to + verb	I'm going to start to save money.

1 Write down the form(s) of the verbs that can follow the verbs below. Then complete
the mottoes. Use the correct form(s) of the verbs given.

1. agree *to + verb*   "Never agree _____ (lend) money to strangers."

2. intend _____   "If you don't intend _____ (do) something properly,

   bother _____   don't bother _____ (start) it!"

3. stop _____   "Never stop _____ (do) the things you

   enjoy _____   enjoy _____ (do)."

4. keep on _____   "Keep on _____ (try) until you find success."

5. consider _____   "Consider _____ (take) every opportunity you get in life."

6. seem _____   "Things aren't always what they seem _____ (be)."

2 *Word builder* Find out the meanings of these verbs, and write down the verb
form(s) that can follow them. Then make up your own motto for each verb.

1. give up _____ _____

2. promise _____ _____

3. put off _____ _____

4. refuse _____ _____

On your own

Make a flip pad for the new verbs you have
learned in this unit. Write each new verb in a
sentence. Every time you have a spare minute,
learn a verb!

Personal tastes

In Unit 2, you learn how to . . .

- make comparisons with *(not) as . . . as.*
- ask negative questions when you want someone to agree.
- talk about fashion and your tastes in clothes and music.
- show understanding by summarizing what people say.
- use *Now* to introduce a follow-up question on a different aspect of a topic.

2

1

4

3

Before you begin . . .
What kind of . . .

- music do you like?
- clothes do you wear?
- car would you like?
- hairstyle suits you?

Do you and your classmates have similiar tastes?

Would you let a friend give YOU a makeover?

We gave Cindy and Ron, two very good friends, the chance to choose
a new look for each other. How did they do? Here's the verdict!

Before

After

**What do you think about
your new look, Cindy?**

I love it! I don't usually
wear these colors, but this
dress is really nice. I like it.
I wouldn't usually wear this
much makeup – I try to get
ready as quickly as I can in
the morning – but it looks
good. I'm really pleased.

**Ron, you chose a completely
different look for Cindy.
How do you like it?**

I like it a lot. I tried as hard
as I could to find a style that
suits her personality better.
Her hair looks great. I mean,
I don't usually like short hair
as much as long hair, but
it suits her, I think. And I
like the dress on her. She
looks great.

Before

After

**How do you like your new
look, Ron?**

Well, I kind of like it. I'm not
used to wearing pants like
these, but they're just as
comfortable as my jeans.
And Cindy made a good
choice with the suede jacket.
It's cool. Yeah, I don't look
as scruffy as I did!

**Cindy, do you like Ron's new
look? He looks very different!**

Yes, I really like it. He doesn't
usually pay much attention to
how he looks – not as much
as he should! Actually, the
pastel shirt I chose doesn't
look as good on him as the
bright colors he usually wears.
I don't think I like pastels that
much after all. But overall, he
looks a lot better! I like his
hair short like that.

1 Getting started

A Look at Cindy's and Ron's "before" and "after" pictures, and listen to their comments.
What do they like about their makeovers? Do you agree with their comments?

*Figure
it out* → **B** How do Cindy and Ron actually say these things? Find the sentences in the article
above. Compare with a partner.

1. *Ron* These pants and my jeans are equally comfortable.
2. *Cindy* Bright colors look better on him than the pastel shirt I chose.
3. *Ron* I usually prefer long hair to short hair.
4. *Ron* I used to look scruffier.

12

2 Grammar Comparisons with (not) as . . . as

Adjectives	The pants are just **as comfortable as** my jeans.
	I don't look **as scruffy as** I did.
Nouns	She spends **as little time as** possible on her makeup.
	She doesn't wear **as many bright colors as** she should.
	He doesn't pay **as much attention** to his appearance **as** he should.
Adverbs	I tried **as hard as** I could to find the right style for her.
	I don't like short hair **as much as** long hair.

About you → **A** Answer these questions with your own opinions. Use *as . . . as* or *not as . . . as*.

1. Are older people just as interested in fashion as young people?
2. Do older people care as much about their appearance as young people?
3. Do men get haircuts as often as women do?
4. Do men spend as much money on themselves as women?
5. Are makeover shows as interesting as other reality shows on TV?
6. When you choose clothes, are looks as important as comfort?
7. Do you have as many clothes as you'd like? How about pairs of shoes?
8. Do you spend as little time as possible shopping for clothes?

B *Group work* Discuss your answers. Explain your views. Do you all agree?

A *It seems to me that older people are just as interested in fashion as young people.*
B *I'm not sure. I don't think older people are as interested.*
C *Well, my mother is a lot more interested in fashion than I am!*

3 Speaking naturally Linking words with the same consonant sound

| bi**g g**lasses | wea**r r**ed | dar**k c**olors | so**me m**akeup | styli**sh sh**oes |

A Listen and repeat the expressions above. Notice that when the same consonant sound is at the end of one word and at the start of the next, it is pronounced once, but it sounds longer.

About you → **B** Now listen and repeat these statements. Are they true for you? Discuss with a partner.

1. I don't like bi**g g**lasses. They're le**ss s**tylish than small glasses.
2. I think people loo**k c**ool in sunglasses.
3. I li**ke c**asual clothes. I can't stan**d d**ressing up for special occasions.
4. I think women should always wear so**me m**akeup.
5. I own a lot of bla**ck c**lothes. I ha**te t**o wear bright colors, and I never wea**r r**ed.
6. I don't usually wear styli**sh sh**oes. They're not as comfortable as my sneakers.

C *Class activity* Ask your classmates questions. Find someone who agrees with each statement.

"Do you like big glasses?"   *"Yes, I do. I think they're just as stylish as small glasses."*

1 Building language

A  Listen. Why doesn't Ben like the jacket? Practice the conversation.

Yoko Oh, don't you just love this jacket?
I mean, isn't it great?

Ben Hmm. I don't know.

Yoko Don't you like it? I think it's really nice.

Ben It's OK. It's kind of bright.

Yoko But don't you like the style? It'd look good
on you, don't you think?

Ben Well, maybe.

Yoko Well, don't you want to try it on at least?

Ben Not really. And anyway, isn't it a little expensive?

Yoko Oh, isn't it on sale?

Ben No. It's full price. The sale rack is over there. Hey,
look at those jackets. Aren't they great?

**Figure
it out** → **B** How does Yoko actually say these things? Underline what she says in the conversation.

1. I love this jacket! 2. I'm surprised you don't like it. 3. I think you should try it on.

2 Grammar *Negative questions*

When you want or expect someone to agree with you, you can use negative questions to:		
Express an opinion	**Suggest an idea**	**Show surprise**
Isn't this jacket great?	**Isn't** it a little expensive?	**Isn't** it on sale?
Don't you think it's great?	**Don't** you think it's too bright?	**Don't** you like it?
Don't you just love it?	It'd look good, **don't** you think?	

▶ *In conversation . . .*

Negative questions with
Isn't . . . ? are the most
common.

Look at the rest of Yoko and Ben's conversation. Rewrite the underlined
sentences as negative questions. Then practice with a partner.

Ben Look at this one. I think it's neat.

Yoko Well, I'm not sure about the style. I think it's a bit boring.

Ben No, I like it. And it fits perfectly, I think.

Yoko Um . . . maybe it's a bit tight.

Ben No, it's just right. I'm surprised you don't like it.
And anyway, it's not as expensive. I think I'll get it!

Yoko Well, I think you should look around a bit more.

Isn't it neat? / Don't you think it's neat?

14

3 Building vocabulary

A *Pair work* Read the product descriptions on this Web page, and take turns describing the items in the photos.

Search

GO

Outerwear

Shirts

Pants

Footwear

Accessories

Activewear

Kids

For Him

For Her

Gift Cards

FREE SHIPPING over $50

1. Choose from our huge selection of men's and women's **leather** and **suede** jackets.

2. Luxury **cashmere** scarves and **silk** ties make perfect gifts.

3. Men's **wool turtleneck** and **V-neck** sweaters.

4. Women's **long-sleeved cotton** tops, available in a range of **solid colors**. Shown here in **neon** green, **dark** green, and **light** green.

5. Looking for **denim** jeans? Whether you want **boot-cut** or **flared, fitted** or **baggy** – we have jeans to fit you!

6. Women's **short-sleeved striped** shirts in **polyester**. **Floral-print** and **plaid** shirts also available.

7. **Rubber** boots in a variety of patterns. Shown here in **turquoise** with a **polka-dot** pattern.

 Word sort

B Complete the chart with words from the Web page, and add ideas. Then compare with a partner. Can you use any of these words to describe what you and your classmates are wearing?

Colors	Patterns	Materials		Styles	
neon green	striped	leather		V-neck	

About you

C *Group work* Talk about the items on the Web page above. Discuss the following questions. Try to use negative questions where possible.

■ Which items do you really like? Are they in style right now?
■ Do you like the colors? How about the materials?
■ Would they look good on you or someone in the group?
■ How much would you pay for them? What would be a reasonable price?

"Isn't that leather jacket great?"   *"I guess so, but don't you think it's a bit out of style?"*

4 Vocabulary notebook *Blue suede shoes*

See page 20 for a useful way to log and learn vocabulary.

He has really broad tastes.

1 Conversation strategy *Summarizing things people say*

A Which response summarizes what A says?

A *A lot of bands sound the same to me. I can't tell one band from another.*
B *I know. _____ .*
   a. They can't play their instruments. b. They sound terrible. c. They're all alike.

Now listen. What do you find out about Omar's brother?

Tracy	So, what are we looking for? I mean, what kind of music does your brother like?
Omar	He likes rock, hip-hop, jazz, . . .
Tracy	Gosh. He has really broad tastes in music.
Omar	Yeah. I'm not sure what to get him. He has hundreds of CDs already.
Tracy	He has a big collection, then.
Omar	Oh, yeah. And he knows a lot about music, too – like song lyrics, what albums are in the charts, when bands had their first hits, . . .
Tracy	Sounds like he's a walking encyclopedia.
Omar	Yeah. He knows everything about this stuff!
Tracy	Now, does he read music magazines? Because you could get him a year's subscription to one.
Omar	Oh, yeah. That's a great idea. I think I'll do that.

Notice how Tracy summarizes the things Omar says. It shows she's involved in the conversation and is following what Omar is saying. Find more examples.

"Gosh. He has really broad tastes in music."

B Match each statement with the best response. Then practice with a partner.

1. I like music with a good rhythm, something catchy. ____
2. I hate listening to music on the radio – they always play the same stuff. ____
3. I like songs that mean something, with words you can remember. ____
4. Rap is really clever, the way it rhymes and tells a story. ____
5. I have every record that The Beatles ever made. ____

a. I know. It's like poetry.
b. Yeah. Good lyrics are important.
c. Wow. That's a big collection.
d. Right. There's not much variety.
e. Uh-huh. You like a good beat.

SELF-STUDY
AUDIO CD
CD-ROM

2 Strategy plus *Now*

Now is often used to introduce a follow-up question. It shows that you want to move the conversation on to a different aspect of a topic.

Now, does he read music magazines?

A Complete the conversations with the questions in the box. Then practice with a partner.

> *In conversation . . .*
>
> *Now* is one of the top 100 words. About 20% of the uses of *now* are to introduce questions.

> do you have satellite radio   do you play any musical instruments
> do you listen to music when you're reading or working

1. *A* Do you like classical music?
   B Yeah. I like most types of music. Classical, jazz, folk – anything, really.
   A So you have pretty broad tastes. Now, _____ ?
   B Not really. I took piano for a while when I was a kid.

2. *A* Do you go to concerts at all?
   B Occasionally. I mean, it's nice to hear live music, but it can get expensive.
   A Yeah, I know. Now, _____ ? They often have live bands.
   B No, I don't have it yet. I don't subscribe to it.

3. *A* Do you have music on all the time at home?
   B Pretty much. It's the first thing I do when I come home – turn on some music.
   A Oh, me too. Now, _____ ?
   B No, I can't have it on when I need to concentrate on something.

About you → **B** Ask and answer the questions. Use your own information.

3 Listening *My music collection*

A Listen to Jason talk to his co-worker about music. Circle the correct information.

1. He owns about **600 / 110** CDs.
2. He plays his CDs in a **normal / special** CD player.
3. He keeps the liner notes about his CDs in **a catalog / the CD cases**.
4. He has copied **some / all** of his CDs onto an MP3 player.
5. He thinks he'll probably **keep / get rid of** his CDs.

B Listen again to excerpts from the conversation. Choose the best response to each one.

1. a. So you have broad tastes.   b. So you're pretty choosy.
2. a. So you have a small collection.   b. So you have a fairly big collection.
3. a. That's enough.   b. That's not nearly enough.
4. a. So it's difficult to use?   b. So it's easy to use, like a jukebox?

17

1 Reading

A Look at the photos of the woman below. What do you think her tastes are in clothes? jewelry? home decor? Make word webs.

miniskirts — clothes   jewelry   home decor

B Read the interview. Were your guesses correct? Do you have anything in common with Lesley? What?

A free spirit!

An interview with Lesley Koustaff in New York about her very individual tastes

How would you describe your style in clothes? Don't you have some pretty unusual clothes?
Yes, I do have some unusual clothes . . . and jewelry! I suppose my style would be called eclectic. I like to collect clothing and jewelry from various countries and combine them. So I suppose the result is an interesting and different look.

Don't you think clothes say a lot about the kind of person you are?
Absolutely. I think we express who we are through our clothes – our personalities are reflected in our clothes.

What do your clothes say about you?
That I am outgoing and an individual – not one of the group. I suppose also that I am creative and a free spirit.

What's your favorite outfit?
My black miniskirt and jacket. I wear it with clunky shoes, lipstick-patterned tights, and very big earrings and a big pin. Jewelry is as important to me as my clothes. I have a handmade shawl made by local people in South Africa that I wear over the jacket.

What kinds of styles and colors don't you wear?
Anything that is very feminine. I don't wear lacy clothes. I love color, so I don't think about whether or not a color looks good on me. I wear every color under the sun . . . sometimes all at once!

What would you never wear?
A backless evening gown and stiletto heels.

What's your taste in music? Don't you have a lot of African music?
Yes, I have a lot of African music – I love the beat and spirit of the music. It comes from the heart. I like to listen to music from a lot of different countries. And I love jazz, classical, and Latin music.

Why don't you tell me about the style of your home? It's so calm in here.
Well, I do *feng shui* – you know, the Chinese art of placing things in harmony – so I took great care in where I placed my furniture. The things I have in my home reflect Africa and Asia, where I spent most of my life, . . . so they are really a part of me, not just items. Each piece has a story. I have a water fountain running 24 hours a day – I love the sound of water and find it very calming.

C Find the underlined words in the interview. What do you think Lesley means when she uses those words? What helped you guess the meaning?

1. Her (clothing) style is <u>eclectic</u>.	a. strange	b. varied	c. exciting
2. Clothes <u>reflect</u> our personalities.	a. show	b. hide	c. develop
3. She is a <u>free spirit</u>.	a. happy	b. sad	c. independent
4. She doesn't like <u>feminine</u> styles.	a. girlish	b. unusual	c. plain
5. She wears every color <u>under the sun</u>.	a. like yellow	b. outdoors	c. that exists

2 Listening and speaking *What's your thing?*

A Listen to four people talk about their tastes. Which two topics does each person talk about?

books   cars   clothes   food   friends   furniture   hairstyles   music

1. Charlie _____ _____   3. Frankie _____ _____
2. Louisa _____ _____   4. Hugo _____ _____

About
you

B Listen again and answer the questions. Who do you have the most in common with? Compare ideas with a partner.

1. Who enjoys reading about his or her interest?   3. Who's not very interested in fashion?
2. Who has simple tastes in food?   4. Who likes to pay more and buy top-quality items?

"I guess I'm a bit like Charlie. You know, I don't like to . . ."

3 Writing and speaking *Style interview*

A Choose a classmate to interview about his or her personal style. Choose five questions from the article on page 18, or make up five of your own. Write them down.

B Exchange questions with your partner. Write answers to your partner's questions.

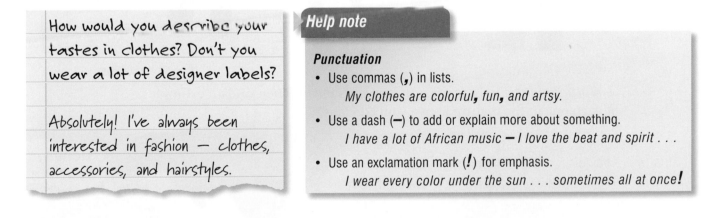

How would you describe your tastes in clothes? Don't you wear a lot of designer labels?

Absolutely! I've always been interested in fashion — clothes, accessories, and hairstyles.

Help note

Punctuation
- Use commas (**,**) in lists.
  *My clothes are colorful**,** fun**,** and artsy.*
- Use a dash (**—**) to add or explain more about something.
  *I have a lot of African music **—** I love the beat and spirit . . .*
- Use an exclamation mark (**!**) for emphasis.
  *I wear every color under the sun . . . sometimes all at once**!***

C *Pair work* Now read your partner's answers. Ask questions to find out more information.

4 Free talk *What's popular?*

See *Free talk 2* at the back of the book for more speaking practice.

Learning tip *Labeling pictures*

When you want to learn a new set of vocabulary, find and label pictures illustrating the new words. For example, you can use a fashion magazine to label items of clothing, styles, colors, patterns, and materials.

Shades of blue

The top ways of describing *blue* in conversation are:

1. *navy* blue   4. *bright* blue
2. *dark* blue   5. *light* blue
3. *royal* blue   6. *deep* blue

1 What styles of clothing, colors, and patterns can you see in the picture? What materials do you think the clothes are made of? Label the picture with words from the box and other words you know.

✓baggy	flared	long-sleeved	silk	turtleneck
cotton	floral-print	neon orange	striped	V-neck
dark brown	leather	polka-dot	✓suede	wool
fitted	light blue	short-sleeved	turquoise	

baggy

suede

2 *Word builder* Find out what these words mean. Then find an example of each one in the picture above, and add labels.

ankle-length	gold	navy blue
beige	maroon	plastic
crew-neck	mauve	tweed

On your own

Find a fashion magazine, and label as many of the different styles, materials, patterns, and colors as you can in ten minutes.

denim, leather, ...

World cultures

In Unit 3, you learn how to . . .

- use the simple present passive to talk about traditional things.
- talk about manners using verb + *-ing* and *to* + verb.
- talk about different cultures and customs.
- use expressions like *in fact* to sound more direct when you speak.
- use *of course* to give information that is not surprising, or to show you understand or agree.

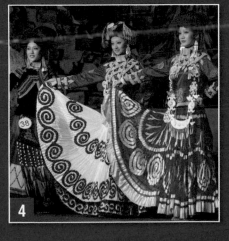

Before you begin . . .

What are some of the cultural traditions in your country? Think of a typical . . .

- dish or drink.
- song or type of music.
- festival.
- costume.
- symbol.
- handicraft.

WHAT **NOT** TO MISS...

We asked people: What's one thing you shouldn't miss on a visit to...?

SOUTH KOREA

"Oh, Korean food! We have so many different dishes. One typical dish is *kim-bap*. It's made with rice and vegetables, and wrapped in dried seaweed. And it's eaten cold. It's delicious."

– Min Hee Park

PERU

"Well, Peru has some beautiful handicrafts. A lot of them are exported nowadays, and they're sold all over the world. But it's still worth visiting a local market. These earrings are made locally. They're made of silver."

– Elena Camacho

JAPAN

"A Japanese festival like the Sapporo Ice Festival – that's really worth seeing. It's held every February. They have all these sculptures that are carved out of ice – and they're carved by teams from all over the world. It's amazing."

– Sachio Ito

AUSTRALIA

"Oh, you should go to a performance of traditional Aboriginal music. They play this instrument – it's called a *didgeridoo*. It's made out of a hollow piece of wood and painted by hand. It makes a really interesting sound."

– Robert Flynn

1 Getting started

A 🔘 Listen to four people talk about their country's culture. What four aspects of culture do they talk about?

> *Figure it out*

B Rewrite the sentences below, but keep the same meaning. Use the comments above to help you.

1. You eat *kim-bap* cold.　　　　　　　　　*Kim-bap* _____ cold.
2. People make earrings like these locally.　Earrings like these _____ locally.
3. They paint *didgeridoos* by hand.　　　　*Didgeridoos* _____ by hand.

2 Grammar *The simple present passive*

Use the passive when the "doer" of the action is not known or not important.

Active	**Passive**
How do they make *kim-bap*?	How **is** *kim-bap* **made**?
They make it with rice and vegetables.	It's **made** with rice and vegetables.
Do they eat it hot or cold?	**Is** it **eaten** hot or cold?
They eat it cold. They don't eat it hot.	It's **eaten** cold. It's not **eaten** hot.
They carve the sculptures out of ice.	The sculptures **are carved** out of ice.

If the "doer" of the action is important, you can introduce it with by.

The sculptures **are carved by** teams from all over the world.

▶ **In conversation . . .**

The most common passive verbs are **made**, **done**, and **called**.

About you ➝ Complete the questions about your country's culture with the simple present passive. Then ask and answer the questions with a partner.

1. What's the national anthem? When ___is it sung___ (sing)?
2. What's your favorite traditional dish? How _____ (make)? What _____ (serve) with?
3. What do you think are the most important festivals? When _____ (celebrate)?
4. Is there a national costume? When _____ (wear)?
5. What are your national sports? _____ (play) by both men and women?
6. Is there any traditional folk music? Where _____ (play)?

"The national anthem is called 'O Canada,' and it's sung at special events."

3 Speaking naturally *Silent syllables*

ev*e*ry   diff*e*rent   int*e*resting   veg*e*table

A 💿 Listen and repeat the words above. Notice how the unstressed vowels are not pronounced

B 💿 Listen to people talk about their cities. Cross out the vowel that is not pronounced in the underlined words. Then read the sentences aloud to a partner.

1. We're known for our <u>choc*o*late</u>, which is sold all over the world. If you're really <u>interested</u>, you can visit a <u>factory</u> to learn about the <u>history</u> of <u>chocolate</u> and how it's made.
2. The <u>average</u> <u>temperature</u> here in summer is almost 40°C, so it's much cooler to live underground. It's definitely something <u>different</u> for <u>travelers</u>!
3. If you want a <u>camera</u>, then you have to shop here. <u>Practically</u> <u>every</u> brand of electronic and computer goods is displayed here!
4. <u>Emeralds</u> are mined all over the world, but our region has some of the best and most <u>valuable</u> stones. They're mostly exported and made into <u>jewelry</u>.

C 💿 Listen again. Can you guess which place each person is talking about? Write the number. What is your region or city known for? Tell the class.

Akihabara, Japan ____   Boyacá, Colombia ____   Broc, Switzerland ____   Coober Pedy, Australia ____

1 Building vocabulary and grammar

A Listen. Are these statements about manners true in your country? Check (✓) true or false.

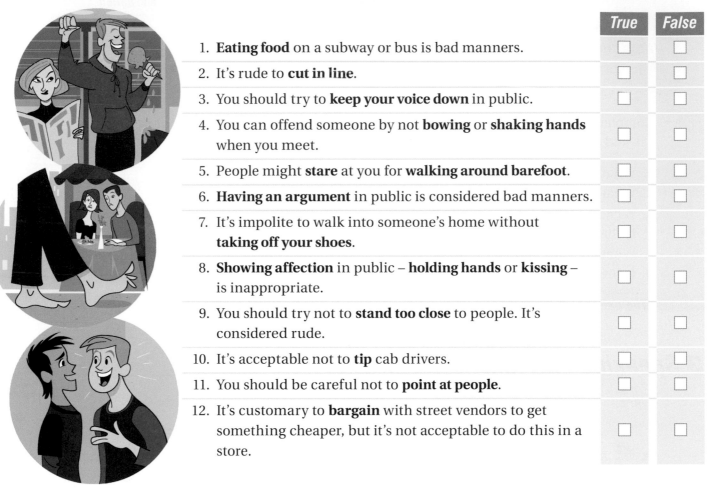

	True	False
1. **Eating food** on a subway or bus is bad manners.	☐	☐
2. It's rude to **cut in line**.	☐	☐
3. You should try to **keep your voice down** in public.	☐	☐
4. You can offend someone by not **bowing** or **shaking hands** when you meet.	☐	☐
5. People might **stare** at you for **walking around barefoot**.	☐	☐
6. **Having an argument** in public is considered bad manners.	☐	☐
7. It's impolite to walk into someone's home without **taking off your shoes**.	☐	☐
8. **Showing affection** in public – **holding hands** or **kissing** – is inappropriate.	☐	☐
9. You should try not to **stand too close** to people. It's considered rude.	☐	☐
10. It's acceptable not to **tip** cab drivers.	☐	☐
11. You should be careful not to **point at people**.	☐	☐
12. It's customary to **bargain** with street vendors to get something cheaper, but it's not acceptable to do this in a store.	☐	☐

Word sort

B What behaviors are considered acceptable in your country? Complete the lists with ideas from above. Add other ideas. Then compare with a partner.

Do . . .	Don't . . .
take your shoes off in the house.	stand too close to people.

Figure it out

C Can you complete these sentences? Use *to* + verb or verb + *-ing*. Compare with a partner.

1. _____ in line is bad manners.
2. You can offend people by _____ affection in public.
3. It's rude not _____ or shake hands when you meet someone.

2 Grammar Verb + -ing and to + verb; position of not 💿

Verb + -ing as a subject
Eating in public is bad manners.
Not shaking hands is impolite.

Verb + -ing after prepositions
You can offend people by **eating** in public.
People might stare at you for **not shaking** hands.

to + verb after It's . . .
It's bad manners **to eat** in public.
It's impolite **not to shake** hands.

Position of not

Not comes before the word it negates.
Be careful **not** to point at people.
You can offend people by **not** bowing.

Notice the difference in meaning:
It's acceptable **not** to tip cab drivers. =
It's optional.
It's **not** acceptable to tip cab drivers. =
You shouldn't do it.

A Complete these sentences about visiting someone's home with either verb + -*ing*
or *to* + verb.

1. It's impolite to go to a friend's home for dinner without
   _____ (bring) a gift.

2. _____ (arrive) a little late is acceptable.

3. It's not a good idea _____ (invite) a friend without
   asking the host.

4. It's polite _____ (compliment) the host's cooking.

5. If you don't like something your host serves, it's best
   _____ (not say) anything and leave it.

6. It's customary _____ (not ask) for second helpings
   of food.

7. _____ (talk) with your mouth full is considered rude.

8. It's acceptable _____ (not finish) the food on your plate.

9. _____ (take) a call on your cell phone during dinner
   is bad manners.

10. You can upset your host by _____ (not leave)
    until it's very late.

About you ➤ **B** *Group work* Discuss the statements above. Which do you agree with?

A I think it's OK not to bring a gift if it's a friend. What do you think?
B Well, actually, I think it's a good idea to bring something, even if it's something small.
C Yeah, I agree. Bringing a gift is good manners.

C *Group work* Can you think of other advice for showing good manners in someone's
home? Make a list to share with the class.

3 Vocabulary notebook Travel etiquette

See page 30 for a new way to log and learn vocabulary.

To be honest, . . .

1 Conversation strategy *Sounding more direct*

A Which of these answers sound more direct? Which sound less direct?

What would you miss about home if you moved abroad?
a. I'd definitely miss my family.
b. I guess I'd miss the people.
c. To be honest, I don't think I'd miss too much.
d. I'd probably miss the culture.

Now listen to Hilda and David. What would David miss if he left Brazil?

Hilda So, when you're living here, do you miss home?

David Um, I don't miss too much, to be honest. Um, I miss my family, of course. . . .

Hilda Right.

David But I definitely don't miss the food! Um, I miss my family. That's about it.

Hilda So, if you went back home, would you miss lots of things about Brazil?

David Oh, yeah. I'd absolutely miss the food here. Yeah. But actually, I think the biggest thing would be . . . it would be weird for me to live in a country where I knew the language already, where all I have to do is work. I just don't see a challenge in that. You know, here every day is a challenge, speaking the language.

Hilda Uh-huh.

David In fact, living back home would be boring, I think. I honestly don't know what I'd do.

Notice that when David wants to sound more direct or assertive, he uses expressions like these. Find examples in the conversation.

absolutely, definitely, really,
actually, certainly, honestly,
in fact, to be honest, to tell you the truth

About you

B Use the expressions given to make these statements more direct. Compare with a partner. Then discuss each statement. Do you agree?

1. If I lived abroad, I'd miss my friends. (definitely)
2. I wouldn't miss the food. (to be honest)
3. I'd enjoy learning a new language. (actually)
4. Shopping would be a challenge. (certainly)
5. I wouldn't be homesick. (to tell you the truth)
6. I wouldn't enjoy living in a different culture. (honestly)

A If I lived abroad, I'd definitely miss my friends!
B Oh, me too. I'd miss everyone, to be honest.

SELF-STUDY
AUDIO CD
CD-ROM

2 Strategy plus *of course*

I miss my family, of course.

Of course usually means "This idea is not surprising. It's what you expect."

You can also use **Of course** in responses to show you agree or understand.

A *I really miss my family.*
B *Of course.*

Note: Be careful when you use *of course*. It can sound abrupt or rude as an answer to a question.

A *Do you miss your family?*
B *Oh, yes, I really do.*
(NOT ~~Of course.~~)

▶ **In conversation . . .**

Of course is one of the top 50 expressions.

A Listen to the questions and answers. Does the expression *of course* in the answer sound polite or impolite? Check (✓) the boxes.

	Polite	Impolite
1. A Do you think living in another country would be exciting? B Absolutely. Of course, I'd probably feel homesick at times.	☐	☐
2. A What would you miss most if you moved to another country? B Well, I'd miss the food and, of course, all my friends.	☐	☐
3. A Would you miss your parents if you were living away from home? B Of course. Wouldn't you?	☐	☐
4. A What would you take with you to remind you of home? B Oh, I'd definitely take my guitar and, of course, all my favorite CDs.	☐	☐
5. A Would you try to learn the language before moving to a new country? B Of course. You really have to learn the language.	☐	☐
6. A How would you keep in touch with everyone? B I'd e-mail regularly, of course, and I'd call them as often as I could.	☐	☐

About you → **B** *Pair work* Ask and answer the questions, giving your own answers. Use *of course* in your answers, but be careful how you use it.

3 Listening and speaking *Away from home*

A Listen to Frances talk about being away from home. How would she answer these questions?

1. Why are you living away from home?
2. Do your parents miss you? Why (not)?
3. How do you keep in touch? How often?
4. What do you miss about home?

About you → **B** *Group work* Think about a time you were away from home. Who and what did you miss? How did you keep in touch? Tell the group about your experience.

"When I went away to college, I really missed my family."

1 Reading

A A popular proverb in English is "Don't count your chickens before they hatch." Can you guess what it means?

B Read the article. Are any of these proverbs familiar to you?

Counting Chickens

The world's timeless proverbs offer great wisdom – which we sometimes turn into folly.

By Fred D. Baldwin

Whenever I find myself banking on future good fortune, I'm apt to think, "Don't count your chickens before they hatch."

Germans express the same idea like this: "You have to catch the hare before you can roast him." The French say: "You can't sell the bear's skin until you've caught him." A Japanese version is almost identical, except that the animal to be caught is a *tanuki*, which resembles a raccoon.

Proverbs – bite-sized chunks of popular wisdom – abound in all languages. We use proverbs to make points more convincingly and more memorably than most of us could otherwise manage. We also use proverbs because they lend a measure of authority to our opinions, suggesting that what we are saying is simply common sense.

Yet proverbial wisdom can be contradictory. We warn the cautious against hesitation with

"He who hesitates is lost," but we also warn the bold, "Look before you leap." We may say that "Absence makes the heart grow fonder," but we also say, "Out of sight, out of mind." When we want help, we say, "Many hands make light work." When we don't want it, we grumble that "Too many cooks spoil the broth."

"Proverbs are not universal truths," says Wolfgang Mieder, professor of German and folklore at the University of Vermont. "Proverbs represent life; therefore, there will be contradictory proverbs."

That proverbs serve as small, prefabricated parts to conversation makes them useful to travelers. If your fluency in a language is limited, a memorized proverb can come in handy when encountering situations likely to occur on any trip – a late arrival, an unexpected turn of events, or perhaps the need to acknowledge a blunder.

I admit, however, to having once spent several uncomfortable minutes in Japan after having come out with "The child of a

frog is a frog," the Japanese version of "The apple doesn't fall far from the tree" – only to be met with blank, uncomprehending stares. It seems that the Japanese word for "frog" sounds much like the Japanese verb "to return." My hosts must have thought that I was babbling about a B movie – something like *The Return of Frog-Boy*.

As we often say, anybody can make a mistake. Or, as a Japanese proverb has it, "Even monkeys fall from trees." When people at the table finally grasped what I was trying to say, my recitation did indeed relax them – doubled them up with laughter, in fact. It gave me a perfect opening for "Fall down seven times, get up eight." That's the Japanese version of "If at first you don't succeed, . . . try, try again."

Fred D. Baldwin enjoyed writing this article, citing the Japanese proverb "To teach is to learn." Baldwin resides in Carlisle, Pennsylvania, U.S.A.

Source: *Attaché* magazine

C Find English proverbs in the article with these meanings. Do you have similar proverbs in your language? Discuss with a partner.

1. Never assume you're going to be lucky.
2. When you miss someone, you love him or her more.
3. Lots of people make a job easier.
4. Never give up.

D Read the article again. Can you find these things? Compare answers with a partner.

1. two reasons why people use proverbs
2. three pairs of proverbs with opposite meanings
3. three situations in which travelers might use proverbs
4. the reason why the author's attempt at using a proverb didn't work
5. a proverb in English and in another language with the same meaning

2 Listening and writing *Favorite proverbs*

A Can you guess the meaning of the proverbs below? Discuss with a partner.

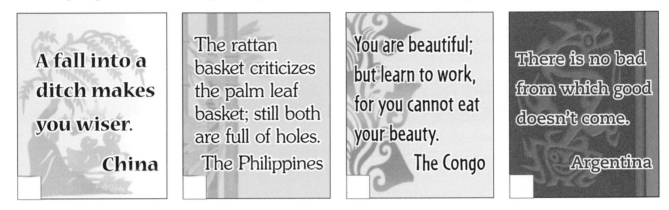

A fall into a ditch makes you wiser. **China**

The rattan basket criticizes the palm leaf basket; still both are full of holes. **The Philippines**

You are beautiful; but learn to work, for you cannot eat your beauty. **The Congo**

There is no bad from which good doesn't come. **Argentina**

B Listen to four people talk about their favorite proverbs. Number the proverbs above.

C Match each proverb above with a similar English proverb below. Write the number. Then listen again as someone responds to each proverb, and check your answers.

a. Every cloud has a silver lining. ___
b. Once bitten, twice shy. ___
c. Beauty is only skin deep. ___
d. It's like the pot calling the kettle black. ___

D What is your favorite proverb? Choose one and write a short article about it. What does it mean? Why do you like it? How does it relate to your life?

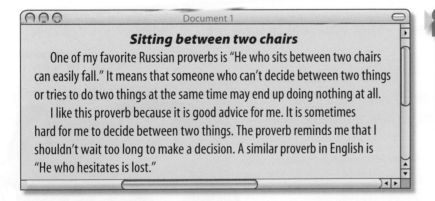

⌐⌐⌐ Document 1

Sitting between two chairs

One of my favorite Russian proverbs is "He who sits between two chairs can easily fall." It means that someone who can't decide between two things or tries to do two things at the same time may end up doing nothing at all.

I like this proverb because it is good advice for me. It is sometimes hard for me to decide between two things. The proverb reminds me that I shouldn't wait too long to make a decision. A similar proverb in English is "He who hesitates is lost."

▶ **Help note**

Useful expressions
One of my favorite proverbs is . . .
It's often said when . . .
It means that . . .
I like it because . . .
A similar proverb in English is ". . ."
The proverb ". . ." expresses the same idea.

E Read your classmates' articles. Which proverb do you think is the most interesting?

3 Free talk *Local customs*

See *Free talk 3* for more speaking practice.

Travel etiquette

When you learn new expressions, try to find more examples in magazines, in newspapers, and on the Internet. To find examples on different Web sites, type the expressions into an Internet search engine, putting quotation marks (" ") around it.

1 Look at the cultural facts about different countries. Complete the sentences using the words and expressions in the box.

to show	to keep your voice down	to take off	bowing	kissing	having an argument
to cut in line	to shake hands	to hold hands	standing	eating	walking around barefoot

1. In Japan, _____ is customary when two people introduce themselves.
2. In the U.S.A., it's polite _____ firmly when you are introduced to a business colleague.
3. In Korea, _____ food on the subway is considered rude.
4. In many places of worship in Asia, it's polite _____ your hat and shoes.
5. In India, it's customary _____ with your friends as you walk together.
6. In Spain, _____ very close to someone when you are talking is acceptable.
7. In Chile, people often say hello by _____ each other on the cheek.
8. In Australia, _____ is acceptable at beach resorts, but not in public buildings.
9. In Saudi Arabia, it's offensive _____ the bottom of your foot to someone.
10. In Taiwan, _____ in public is considered impolite. It's better _____ .
11. In Great Britain, it's considered rude _____ . You should always wait your turn.

2 *Word builder* Find out the meaning of these words and expressions. Then write a real etiquette tip about each for your culture.

blow your nose   **burp**   **offer your seat to someone**   **swear**

Choose a country you would like to visit. Find a travel guide on that country, or go on the Internet. Make a list of 6 things you should or shouldn't do when you travel there.

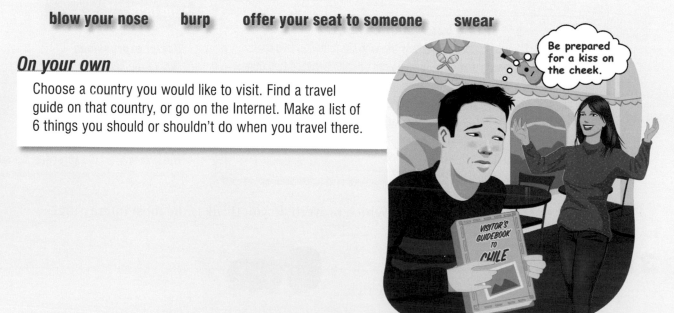

Be prepared for a kiss on the cheek.

1 Is it polite?

A Complete the questions with the correct forms of the verbs.

1. Would you ever consider ____not tipping____ (not tip) a server in a restaurant?
2. Do you remember _____ (stare) at people when you were little?
3. Do you feel it's rude _____ (not say) hello to your neighbors?
4. Is _____ (hold hands) OK on a first date?
5. Do you bother _____ (bargain) with street vendors when the items are already very cheap?
6. Do you ever offer _____ (help) people on the bus or subway with their bags?
7. Have you and a friend ever ended up _____ (argue) in public?
8. Have you ever offended someone without _____ (intend) _____ (be) rude?

B *Pair work* Ask and answer the questions. Show that you understand your partner's answers by summarizing what he or she says.

"I'd never consider not tipping – I used to be a server myself."   *"So you always tip the server."*

2 Think, Bob, think!

A Complete the conversation with the correct forms of the verbs.

Officer __Have__ you __seen__ (see) these people before?

Bob Yes, they're my neighbors. They _____ (live) upstairs.

Officer How long _____ they _____ (live) there?

Bob I guess I _____ (know) them for six months. They _____ (move) here in August.

Officer When _____ you last _____ (see) them?

Bob Um, about a week ago, I think. Last Tuesday.

Officer What _____ they _____ (do) when you _____ (see) them?

Bob Well, as I _____ (come) home, they _____ (carry) a big suitcase to the car.

Officer _____ you _____ (speak) to them?

Bob I _____ (say), "Hi! Where _____ you _____ (go)?" And they _____ (reply), "On vacation."

Officer What time _____ they finally_____ (leave)?

Bob Oh, um, it was pretty late, around 11 at night, I guess.

Officer Can you remember what they _____ (wear)?

Bob Let me think. . . .

B Write Bob's answer to the police officer's last question. How much detail can you give? Compare with a partner.

3 Can you complete this conversation?

A Complete the conversation with the words and expressions in the box. Practice the conversation.

✓definitely	don't you think	now	of course	these	this	to be honest

Anna Bella used to live in Japan. You loved living there, right?

Bella Oh, __definitely__ . I lived there for nine years, working for a Japanese advertising company.

Chris Nine years? Wow! Didn't you ever get homesick?

Bella Occasionally. But, _____ , I didn't really miss living at home. I was too busy. I mean, _____ I missed my family.

Chris Oh, I bet you did. _____ , how did you get that job? Did they hire you over here, or . . . ?

Bella Actually, I was already in Japan on an exchange program, staying with _____ family. And the father starts bringing home all _____ documents from his work to translate into English. Anyway, I started helping him, and his company ended up hiring me.

Anna And they transferred her here. It's a cool story, _____ ?

B *Pair work* Choose a topic and have a conversation. Ask and answer questions.

- something difficult you did once
- an interesting experience you had
- a time you missed someone
- an unusual person you once met

4 As bad as that?

Pair work Compare these things using *(not) as . . . as.* Try to use negative questions to give opinions or to suggest ideas.

- folk music / rock music
- baked potatoes / fries
- old buildings / new buildings
- cheap watches / expensive watches

A **Folk music isn't as popular as rock music. You don't hear it as much.**

B **But don't you think it's just as good? I like folk as much as rock.**

5 Guess the dish!

A Write questions in the simple present passive, using these words. Then think of a traditional dish, and answer the questions.

1. eat / hot or cold
2. When / eat
3. How / cook
4. What / make / with
5. What / serve / with
6. What / call

B *Pair work* Take turns asking and answering the questions. Can you guess your partner's dish before question 6?

Self-check

How sure are you about these areas? Circle the percentages.

grammar
20% 40% 60% 80% 100%

vocabulary
20% 40% 60% 80% 100%

conversation strategies
20% 40% 60% 80% 100%

. . . .

Study plan

What do you want to review? Circle the lessons.

grammar
1A 1B 2A 2B 3A 3B

vocabulary
1A 1B 2A 2B 3A 3B

conversation strategies
1C 2C 3C

Socializing

In Unit 4, you learn how to . . .

- talk about things you *are supposed to* do.
- use *was / were supposed to* and *was / were going to* to talk about things you didn't do.
- talk about going out and socializing.
- use different expressions with the verb *get*.
- use questions in the form of statements to check your understanding.
- use *so* in different ways, such as to start or close a topic.

Before you begin . . .

Where are some good places to go out with friends?

Is it expensive to go out in your city?

Who do you usually socialize with?

Marco: Are you going to Brad and Gayle's party?

Marco: Well, I wasn't going to go, but maybe I will. I'm supposed to be studying for an exam. Are you going?

Anna: Yeah. The party's at their house, right? Do you know where they live?

Anna: Not exactly. Brad was going to call and give me directions, but he didn't. Maybe Ellen knows.

Ellen: What kind of party is it?

Ellen: I think it's supposed to be a barbecue.

Phil: That'll be fun. Have you heard the weather forecast?

Phil: Yeah. I heard it's supposed to be a really nice evening.

Anwar: Are we supposed to bring anything?

Sue: I don't think so. I was going to make some potato salad, but I didn't have time.

Anwar: Well, I bought them a box of chocolates. Do you think that'll be OK?

Sue: I don't know. Isn't Brad on a diet? He's not supposed to eat stuff like that. But Gayle will like them.

Patty: Jen and Martin are late. They were supposed to pick me up at 7:00.

Junko: Gosh, it's 7:30 already. Maybe they forgot. Do you want me to come and get you? I can take you home, too.

Patty: That'd be great. But I'm supposed to be at work early tomorrow, so I can't stay late.

Junko: That's OK. I think the party's supposed to end at 11:00, but we can leave a bit earlier.

1 Getting started

A 🔘 Listen. Brad and Gayle are having a party tonight, and their friends are getting ready. What do you find out about the party?

Figure it out

B How might Brad and Gayle's friends say the things below? Replace the underlined words with an expression each person has already used above.

1. *Phil* They say it's going to be really warm.
2. *Sue* Brad shouldn't eat chocolate.
3. *Patty* I have to get up early tomorrow.
4. *Anna* I should be working on a paper.
5. *Patty* Jen and Martin agreed to be here by 7:00.
6. *Sue* I intended to make a dessert, but I didn't.

2 Grammar *be supposed to; was / were going to*

Be supposed to *can mean "They say . . . ."*	It's **supposed to** be a barbecue. It's **supposed to** rain later.
It can also mean "have to" or "should."	I'm **supposed to** work tomorrow. He's **not supposed to** eat chocolate.
It can contrast what should happen with what does or will happen.	I'm **supposed to** be studying for an exam (but I'm not). I'm **not supposed to** stay out late (but maybe I will).
Was / Were supposed to *can mean what was expected didn't or won't happen.*	They **were supposed to** come at 7:00 (but they didn't). I **wasn't supposed to** go by myself (but I'll have to).
Was / Were going to *has a similar meaning and can also mean "intended to."*	He **was going to** give us directions (but he didn't). I **wasn't going to** go to the party (but I guess I will).

In conversation . . .

Over 60% of uses of **supposed to** are in the present tense. About 10% are negative.

A Complete the conversations with the correct form of *be supposed to* or *was / were going to* and the verb. Sometimes more than one answer is possible. Practice with a partner.

1. *A* Are there any restaurants around here that _____ (be) really good?

    B Yeah, the new Turkish one around the corner _____ (be) excellent. And there's a good Italian restaurant two blocks away. We _____ (go) there last Friday, but I had to work late.

2. *A* The weather _____ (be) beautiful this weekend. Do you have any plans?

    B Yeah, I _____ (go) to my parents' house. They're planning a surprise party for my birthday, and I _____ (not / know) about it, but my sister told me about it last week.

3. *A* How was your weekend? Did you do anything fun?

    B Not really. My friend _____ (come) and have dinner at my place, and then we _____ (see) a movie, but she got sick and couldn't make it. How about you?

    A Well, I _____ (not / do) anything because I had to study, but I went out anyway.

About you → **B** *Pair work* Ask and answer the questions. Give your own answers.

3 Talk about it *Weekend fun*

Group work Discuss the questions about this weekend.

► What's the weather supposed to be like?
► Are there any upcoming events that are supposed to be fun?
► Are there any new movies that are supposed to be good?
► Are you supposed to go anywhere or see anyone in particular?
► Is there anything you were going to do last weekend that you're going to do this weekend instead?

We've got to get going.

1 Building vocabulary and grammar

A  Listen. Where are Luis and Rosa going? Do they want to go? Practice the conversation.

Luis Rosa, it's 6:00. We're supposed to be there by 7:00. Weren't you supposed to **get off** work early today?

Rosa Well, my boss called a meeting, and I couldn't **get out of** it. I had to go. Anyway, I don't **get it** – why is your cousin getting married on a Friday and not a Saturday, like everyone else?

Luis I don't know. All I know is that my mother will never **get over** it if we walk in late. So we have to **get going**.

Rosa OK. Uh, do you think I can **get away with** wearing pants?

Luis No way! It's supposed to be a formal wedding. Look, I got your silk dress ready for you.

Rosa Oh, I'll never **get used to** dressing up for these fancy weddings. Can we try to **get home** early?

Luis Rosa, I **get the feeling** that you don't really want to go.

Rosa Well, I just hope I can **get through** the reception.

Luis Oh, come on. Let's just go and enjoy it. It's a chance for you to **get to know** my family better. By the way, did you **get around to** buying a gift?

Rosa Weren't *you* supposed to do that?

Word sort ➔ **B** Find a *get* expression from the conversation above to complete each example sentence below. Are the sentences true for you? Compare with a partner.

	get expression	Example sentences
1.	get off	I usually __get off__ work early on Fridays. I leave at about 3:00.
2.	_____	I don't like to stay at work late. I always try to _____ by 5:30 to cook dinner.
3.	_____	I was so busy last week that I didn't _____ doing my homework.
4.	_____	I'm usually late, so my friends are always saying, "We have to _____ ."
5.	_____	Sometimes I _____ that people are annoyed with me for being late.
6.	_____	I like going out after class. It's a chance to _____ my classmates.
7.	_____	It's hard for me to finish long novels. I just can't _____ them.
8.	_____	I don't know why people dress up for weddings. I just don't _____ .
9.	_____	I'll never _____ wearing formal clothes. They don't feel right.
10.	_____	I wish I could _____ wearing jeans all the time. They're so comfortable.

Figure it out ➔ **C** Can you put the words in the right order to complete the sentences? Compare with a partner.

1. Rosa had to attend a meeting at work. She couldn't _____ (out / it / get / of).

2. Luis's mother will be upset if they're late. She'll never _____ (it / over / get).

2 Grammar *Inseparable phrasal verbs* 💿

> **With these verbs, the object always comes after the particle or preposition.**
>
> **Verb + particle + object**
> Weren't you supposed to **get off** work early?
> She'll never **get over** feeling embarrassed.
>   I'm sure she'll **get over** it.
> I hope I can **get through** the reception.
>   I know you can **get through** it.
>
> **Verb + particle + preposition + object**
> Can I **get away with** wearing pants?
>   No. You can't **get away with** it.
> Couldn't you **get out of** the meeting?
>   No, I couldn't **get out of** it.
> Did you **get around to** buying a gift?
>   No, I never **got around to** it.

About you → Complete the questions. Put the words in order, and use the correct form of the verbs. Then ask and answer the questions with a partner.

1. If you had an important date, would you try to <u>get out of coming</u> (get / of / come / out) to class? Would you ask if you could _____ (off / work / get) early?
2. Do you find it hard to _____ (the week / through / get) if you don't have time to go out with friends?
3. Do you have any shy friends who are always trying to _____ _____ (of / get / go / out) to parties? What can they do to _ _____ (get / their shyness / over)?
4. Have you ever told a "white lie" to _____ (of / get / an invitation / out)? Did you _____ (get / it / away / with)?
5. How quickly can you _____ (through / get / your e-mail)? Does it take you a long time to _____ (answer / to / get / around) e-mail from friends?
6. How do you feel about buying gifts? Does it take you a long time to _____ _____ (to / get / it / around)?

3 Speaking and listening *What are you like?*

About you → **A** Look at the sentences below. Which choice is most like you? Tell a partner.

---

1 I'm one of those people who …
  a. gets ready at the last minute.
  b. spends ages getting ready.

2 If I'm late for something, I usually …
  a. hurry to try to be on time.
  b. take my time and arrive late.

3 When I go out, I always …
  a. make an effort to dress up.
  b. try and get away with wearing jeans.

4 If a friend cancels plans we made, …
  a. I stay home and feel disappointed.
  b. I get over it and do something else instead.

B 💿 Listen to Paula and Roberto talk about their plans for tonight. What happens?

C 💿 Listen again. How would Roberto complete the sentences above? Circle his choices.

4 Vocabulary notebook *Get this!*

See page 42 for a useful way to log and learn vocabulary.

Lesson C   So, it's your birthday?

1 Conversation strategy *Checking your understanding*

A How are the two questions in this conversation different?

A *So, um, are you going out tonight?*   A *You're going out with Karl?*
B *Yes, I'll probably meet Karl.*   B *Yeah.*

Now listen. What does Martin usually do on his birthday?

Grant	**So, it's your birthday Friday, right?**
Martin	**Yeah, but I've never made a big deal about it. It's been a long time since I've had a party or anything.**
Grant	**What if somebody planned a surprise party?**
Martin	**One time my wife did. We were talking and I said, "You know, this year for my birthday, let's just hang out, rent a movie." And she got really quiet.**
Grant	**Oh, really? When you said that?**
Martin	**Yeah. Then she said, "I invited all your old friends over." And I said, "Well, they're my <u>old</u> friends for a reason." It was a disaster.**
Grant	**So they all came, huh?**
Martin	**Yeah. They all came, so . . .**

Notice how Grant checks his understanding. He asks questions in the form of statements. People often add *huh* or *right* at the end of questions like these. Find more examples.

"So, it's your birthday Friday, right?"

B Read more of their conversation. Change Grant's questions to "statement questions." Then listen and notice what Grant actually says.

Grant So, was it supposed to be a surprise? 1. <u>So, it was supposed to be a surprise?</u>
        And did you know about it? 2. _____
Martin Yeah. I already knew.
Grant Was the party the next day? 3. _____
Martin No, it was probably like a week later.
Grant Oh, so did you have a week to feel bad about it? 4. _____
Martin Yeah. I had a whole week to think about it.
Grant So did you really hate the party? 5. _____
Martin Well, kind of. I mean, it was really sweet of her to do that, but . . .

SELF-STUDY
AUDIO CD
CD-ROM

2 Strategy plus *so*

You can use **SO** in many ways, including:

To start a topic, often with a question
So, it's your birthday Friday, right?

To check your understanding
So they all came, huh?

To pause or let the other person draw a conclusion
They all came, so . . .

To close a topic
So that's what happened. They all came.

So they all came, huh?

A Find three places where you can use *so* in each conversation. Change the capital letters and add commas where necessary. Then practice with a partner.

In conversation . . .

So is one of the top 20 words.

1. *A* <u>So,</u> W̌hat do you think of surprise parties?
   B ___ I don't know. I've never had one or been to one.
   A ___ No one ever gave you one? Do you think your friends would ever do that?
   B ___ No. My friends don't do that kind of thing. ___ Probably not.

2. *A* ___ Has anyone ever given you a gift as a surprise, for no reason?
   B ___ Actually, yes. My friend gave me this great book. ___ I didn't expect it.
   A ___ It wasn't for your birthday or anything?
   B ___ No, she just gave it to me because she wanted to, ___ . . .

3. *A* ___ Have you been to any good parties lately?
   B ___ Well, I've been very busy at work recently, ___ . . .
   A ___ You haven't been going out too often, then?
   B ___ No, I guess not.

About you → **B** *Pair work* Ask and answer the questions. Give your own answers.

3 Speaking naturally *Being sure or checking*

If you are sure: So your birthday's on Friday.
So all your friends came.

If you are checking: So your birthday's on Friday?
So all your friends came?

A Listen and repeat the sentences. Notice how the intonation falls when you say something you are sure about, and rises when you're checking information.

B Listen to four conversations. Are the speakers sure, or are they checking? Add a period or a question mark, and write *S* or *C*.

1. So you go out a lot ___
2. So you're a real people person ___
3. So you don't like parties very much ___
4. So you never celebrate your birthday ___

1 Reading

A Are you an extrovert? Do you enjoy socializing and meeting new people? Or are you more of an introvert, someone who prefers to spend time alone? Tell the class.

B Read the article. What's Marti Olsen Laney's book about?

Socializing the introvert

A confirmed introvert says it's OK to be that way. She should know. She's a psychologist who has written a book on the subject. *By Jenny Yuen*

As an introvert, Marti Olsen Laney knows how difficult it can be to socialize. She sometimes heads straight for the bathroom the second she arrives at a party. But she's not exactly paralyzed in a crowd. In fact, the California psychologist seemed entirely at ease last week as she addressed about 20 people who turned out for her discussion of the introverted personality. Perhaps predictably, those in the audience did not sit close to each other. But that's OK. Really. The author of *Introvert Advantage* revealed that being introverted is quite normal. "We've all grown up in an extroverted society," Olsen Laney said. "There really is quite a concept of negativity attached to introverts."

Thinking outside the box

Many people prefer to spend time alone, work better independently than in group settings, and cherish celebrating birthdays with close friends rather than with large groups. This introverted personality is often stereotyped as unstable, lonely, and antisocial, but Olsen Laney said there are many advantages to being introverted.

She said introverts are likely to be resilient, determined, good listeners, creative thinkers, and very knowledgeable about themselves. "Introverts think outside the box. They also express themselves better in writing than in speech," Olsen Laney said.

Behavior often mistaken for aloofness

Introversion may affect one's family life if there is a clash of extroverted parents with introverted kids. It may also impact one's career if a boss does not think an introverted employee contributes enough, because introverts tend to keep information to themselves. This behavior is often mistaken for aloofness.

"If you just ask them, it's amazing what ideas they'll tell you," she said.

Still, Olsen Laney said there are ways for introverts to cope with uncomfortable social functions without mentally breaking down. She said they can be social at events where there is interesting conversation, but not when it's a party that they feel is meaningless.

"Introverted people don't like to be interrupted because it's hard to find your train of thought again," she said. "A lot of the reasons introverted people are seen the way they are is because chitchat is totally unrewarding for our system."

Being introverted in an extroverted world

Olsen Laney recommended that introverts restore body energy by taking breaks and spending quiet time alone to shut out extra stimuli so they don't become overwhelmed or feel the need to change themselves.

"All introverts have to be extroverted in their life without having to change completely," she said. "It's important to find the balance of having an occupation where you can be extroverted and still have time for yourself."

Source: *Toronto Observer*

C Can you find words or expressions in the article that mean these things? Underline them.

1. unable to move or speak
2. thinking creatively
3. able to get over things easily
4. unfriendliness
5. a conflict between
6. have an effect on
7. remember what you were thinking
8. small talk

D Read the article again, and answer the questions. Then compare your answers with a partner.

1. Is Marti Olsen Laney an extrovert or an introvert?
2. How do introverts generally feel about working or socializing in groups?
3. What are some good qualities that introverts can have?
4. What are some problems that introverts encounter in society?
5. Why are introverted people often not comfortable at parties?
6. How does Marti Olsen Laney advise introverts to cope with life in an extroverted society?

2 Listening and writing *Extrovert or introvert?*

About you

A *Group work* Take the magazine quiz, and discuss the questions. How are you the same?

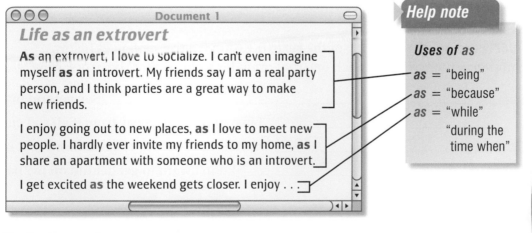

What's your social style?

Do you prefer to . . .		ANSWERS	
		Me	Jun

EXTROVERT	INTROVERT		
1. a. go out and socialize?	b. see friends at home?	**1.** a b	a b
2. a. have lots of friends?	b. have just a few close friends?	**2.** a b	a b
3. a. go out in a big group?	b. go out with one or two friends?	**3.** a b	a b
4. a. be the center of attention?	b. keep a low profile?	**4.** a b	a b
5. a. tell jokes and stories?	b. listen as other people tell jokes?	**5.** a b	a b
6. a. engage in chitchat?	b. have more serious conversations?	**6.** a b	a b
7. a. do tasks with others?	b. figure things out alone?	**7.** a b	a b
8. a. think of yourself as a "social animal"?	b. think of yourself as an individual?	**8.** a b	a b

B Listen to Jun talk about his social life. How would he answer the quiz? Circle his answers.

C Write a short article about your social style. Are you an introvert, an extrovert, or a little of both?

○○○   Document 1

Life as an extrovert

As an extrovert, I love to socialize. I can't even imagine myself **as** an introvert. My friends say I am a real party person, and I think parties are a great way to make new friends.

I enjoy going out to new places, **as** I love to meet new people. I hardly ever invite my friends to my home, **as** I share an apartment with someone who is an introvert.

I get excited **as** the weekend gets closer. I enjoy . . .

▶**Help note**

Uses of as

as = "being"

as = "because"

as = "while" "during the time when"

D *Group work* Read your classmates' articles. Have they supported their points with clear examples? Can you offer suggestions to improve their writing?

3 Free talk *Pass on the message.*

See *Free talk 4* for more speaking practice.

Get this!

Learning tip Expressions in context

When you learn a new expression, write an example sentence that uses it in context. Think of something you might want to say, and add ideas that set the scene or help you remember its meaning.

> **Get into it!**
>
> The top 10 particles and prepositions after **get** are:
>
> 1. out   6. up
> 2. into   7. on
> 3. in   8. away
> 4. to   9. off
> 5. back   10. down

1 Complete the sentences using a *get* expression from the box.

get away with it	get it	get out of it	get to know
get going	get off	get over it	get used to

1. I'm late. I'd better _____ .

2. I love meeting new people. I think it's a lot of fun to _____ people.

3. Weekends seem so short. I wish I could _____ work early every Friday.

4. You're not supposed to go into clubs under the age of 18, but I know some kids manage to _____ .

5. I'll never _____ wearing a suit to work.

6. I don't understand why some people stay home all the time. I just don't _____ .

7. I was going to go to my class reunion. But I've decided to try and _____ .

8. When I failed the exam, I thought I would never _____ , but actually, I'm enjoying taking this class again.

2 Word builder Find out the meaning of the *get* expressions in the sentences below. Then write another sentence before each one that provides a context for the expression.

1. _____ She **gets on my nerves**.

2. _____ I just need to **get away from it all** so I can relax.

3. _____ Maybe there's a way to **get around** that problem.

4. _____ I don't want to **get behind on** my payments.

On your own

Get a flip pad. Make different sections for common verbs like *get*, *go*, *do*, and *have*. Write as many expressions as you can for each verb.

Law and order

In Unit 5, you learn how to . . .

- use the passive of modal verbs.
- use the *get* passive.
- talk about rules and regulations, crime and punishment.
- organize your views with expressions like *First of all, Basically,* etc.
- use expressions like *That's a good point* to show someone has a valid argument.

Before you begin . . .

Do you have laws about these things in your country? What are they?

- wearing seat belts and using a cell phone in a car
- at what age you can ride a motorcycle and what you have to wear
- how you should get rid of litter or garbage

Rules and regulations

The Age of **Majority**

In many countries, the law permits you to engage in new activities at the age of 18. We asked people what they think about 18 as the "age of majority."

When you turn 18, you can go see an "R-rated" movie – a movie that's restricted to adults. What do you think about that?

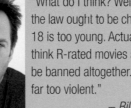

"What do I think? Well, I think the law ought to be changed – 18 is too young. Actually, I think R-rated movies should be banned altogether. They're far too violent."

– Bill Hughes

Do you think you should be able to get married before you're 18?

"No way. In fact, you shouldn't be allowed to get married until you're at least 21 or even older. Then there might be fewer divorces. Actually, I think a law should be passed that says if you want to get married, you have to take marriage classes first!"

– Maya Diaz

Do you think you should be allowed to vote at 18?

"I guess. I mean, you can do everything else at 18. Why not vote? It's too bad more young people don't vote, though. I think everyone should be made to vote."

– Aiko Niwano

You can get your own credit card at the age of 18. Is this too young?

"I don't think so. I mean, young people have to be given their freedom at some point. You know, they ought to be encouraged to manage their own finances and things. They can always learn from their mistakes."

– Jared Blake

The legal age for most things is 18, but in many places you can drive at 16. Is that a good idea, do you think?

"I must say I've always thought 16 is too young. Too many teenagers get involved in traffic accidents, and something really must be done about it. The legal age for driving could easily be changed to 18 or 21 or something like that."

– Pat Johnson

1 Getting started

A 🔘 Listen to these interviews. What five things do the people talk about? Do they think 18 is the right age to start doing these things? What are the laws in your country?

Figure it out ➔

B How do the people above say these things? Find the sentences in the article, and underline them. Do you agree with these views? Discuss with a partner.

1. They should ban R-rated movies.
2. They shouldn't allow you to get married until you're 21.
3. They should make everyone vote.
4. They ought to encourage young people to manage their own finances.
5. They could easily change the legal age for driving to 18.

2 Grammar *The passive of modal verbs*

> **Modal verb + be + past participle**
>
> R-rated movies **should be banned**.   The legal age **could** easily **be changed**.
> You **shouldn't be allowed** to marry at 18.   Something **must be done** about it.
> They **have to be given** their freedom.   The law **ought to be changed**.

A Read these views about different laws. Rewrite the sentences starting with the words given.

1. They must do something about junk e-mail. Something . . .
   Something must be done about junk e-mail.
2. They ought to arrest people for sending spam. People . . .
3. They have to do something about all the litter on the buses and in subways. Something . . .
4. They shouldn't allow people to eat food on public transportation. People . . .
5. They ought to fine people for making noise after midnight. People . . .
6. They shouldn't allow people to buy fireworks. People . . .
7. They should ban all movies with violent scenes. All movies . . .
8. They could encourage people to stop smoking if there were more anti-smoking laws. People . . .
9. They could easily ban smoking in all public places – nobody would complain. Smoking . . .
10. They shouldn't allow children to quit school until they are 18. Children . . .

> **In conversation . . .**
>
> **Must** means "have to" in 10% of its uses. In this meaning, it is often used in expressions like **I must admit** and **I must say**.
>
> 90% of the uses of **must** are for speculation:
> **Things must be hard for couples who marry young.**

About you → **B** *Pair work* Discuss the sentences with a partner. Which statements do you agree with?

A *I agree that something must be done about junk e-mail.*
B *Absolutely. I think spam ought to be totally banned. It wastes too much time.*

3 Speaking naturally *Saying conversational expressions*

> *I mean, you can do everything else at 18. Why not vote? You know what I mean?*
> *You know, they ought to be encouraged to manage their own finances and things.*
> *The legal age for driving could easily be changed to 18 or 21 or something like that.*

A Listen and repeat the sentences above. Notice how the expressions in bold are said more quickly, even when the speaker is speaking slowly.

About you → **B** *Group work* Discuss the questions in the interviews on page 44. Then decide on . . .

■ three laws that should be passed.
■ three things that people should be encouraged to do.
■ three things that people ought to be allowed to do.

Crime and punishment

What punishment best fits the crime?

Here are some opinions from readers of *The Daily Gazette*.

❶ "I think **shoplifters** should be **fined** at first, but if they get caught **stealing** again and again, they should go to **jail**."

❷ "I don't know. Some people get **sentenced** to only 10 or 15 years for **murder**. **Killing** another person is the worst crime, but it's a complex issue."

❸ "That depends. If you commit **armed robbery**, you know, use a **gun** or a **knife**, you should be sent to prison."

❹ "**Taking** someone **captive** and asking for money is a major crime. **Kidnappers** should go to prison for a long time."

❺ "If the **vandalism** isn't too serious, they should just have to clean up their **graffiti**, or pay for any damage."

❻ "**Breaking into** someone's home is serious. But first-time **burglars** should just be **put on probation**."

❼ "You don't usually get **arrested** for speeding unless you cause an accident, and that seems fair. But if you get stopped a lot, you should **lose your license**."

❽ "A **fine**, maybe? I know it's **against the law** to just cross the street anywhere, but it's a relatively minor **offense**. And the law doesn't get **enforced** much."

1 Building vocabulary and grammar

A Read the opinions from readers in the newspaper above. What questions are they answering? Number the questions below. Then listen and check your answers.

| 8 | What's the right **penalty** for **jaywalking**? |

| | Should they **arrest** drivers who get caught **speeding**? |

| | What should happen if you get caught **shoplifting** from a store? |

| | How should **vandals** be **punished**? |

| | What punishment should you get for **robbing** someone? |

| | What should happen to someone who is **convicted** of **burglary**? |

| | What kind of **sentence** should you get for **kidnapping**? |

| | Should all **murderers** be sentenced to **life in prison**? |

Word sort → **B** Complete the chart. Then describe each crime or offense to a partner. Which do you think are major crimes? Which are minor offenses?

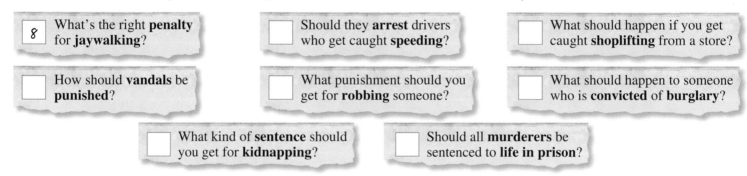

crime / offense	shoplifting		vandalism		burglary		murder
person	shoplifter	jaywalker		robber		kidnapper	

"Shoplifting is when you steal things from a store. I think it's a relatively minor offense."

Figure it out → **C** What happens to people in your country when they break the law? Complete the sentences with expressions from the article. Then compare with a partner.

1. People who commit murder usually get _____ .
2. If you get caught shoplifting, you usually get _____ .
3. If a person commits burglary for the first time, he or she gets _____ .

2 Grammar *get passive vs. be passive* 💿

Examples of get passive
People who speed don't usually **get arrested**.
Some murderers **get sentenced** to only 10 years.

After should, the be passive is more common.
People who speed should **be arrested** if they cause an accident.
Some murderers should **be sentenced** to life in prison.

Notice:
catch + verb + -ing
What happens if they **catch** you **shoplifting**?
What happens if you get **caught shoplifting**?

▶ *In conversation . . .*

People use the **get** passive much more frequently in speaking than in writing.

A Complete the comments about law enforcement. Use the *get* passive or *be* passive with the verb given.

1. "Vandalism should _____ (punish) more severely. Vandals should _____ (sentence) to a month of community service."
2. "More shoplifters _____ (catch) these days because of all the cameras they have in stores. Just the same, most shoppers are honest, and they really shouldn't _____ (videotape)."
3. "People who speed hardly ever _____ (stop) by the police. The laws against speeding should _____ (enforce) more strictly."
4. "Lots of executives _____ (catch) stealing from their companies, but they _____ (not send) to prison for very long. It doesn't seem right."
5. "A big problem is that most criminals never _____ (catch), and the ones that _____ (arrest) often _____ (not convict)."
6. "People under 18 shouldn't _____ (give) a prison sentence if they commit a crime. They should just _____ (put) on probation."

About you → **B** *Pair work* Discuss the statements and opinions above. Do you agree?

C *Group work* Discuss the questions from Exercise 1A on page 46. Do you all agree?

3 Listening *We got robbed!*

A 💿 Listen to Jenny talk about a burglary. Answer the questions.

1. When did the burglary happen?
2. Who discovered it and how?
3. What did the burglars take?
4. Did the burglars get caught?

B 💿 Listen again. How does Jenny feel about the burglary? Check (✓) the sentences.

☐ She never expected it to happen.
☐ She was scared.
☐ She thinks it was funny.
☐ She feels she was luckier than many people.
☐ She was very angry and upset.
☐ She thinks it was inconvenient.

4 Vocabulary notebook *It's a crime!*

See page 52 for a new way to log and learn vocabulary.

1 Conversation strategy *Organizing your views*

A Imagine you are giving your views about something. In what order could you use these expressions to organize what you say?

_____ *Second*   _____ *Another thing is*   _____ *First of all*

Now listen. What do Jin Ho and Celia think of security cameras?

Jin Ho   *What do you think of all these security cameras they have now?*

Celia   *Well, basically I'm in favor of them.*

Jin Ho   *You are?*

Celia   *Yeah. I mean, for two reasons. First, they're like a deterrent – you're not going to commit a crime if you know you're being filmed on camera, and secondly, they help the police catch criminals.*

Jin Ho   *Well, that's true. But on the other hand, don't you think they're a bit intrusive?*

Celia   *But if you're not doing anything wrong, what's the problem?*

Jin Ho   *Well, that's a good point, but some people would say it's an invasion of privacy – someone watching you all the time.*

Celia   *I guess. I must admit, I never thought of it that way.*

Notice how Celia organizes what she says by using expressions like these. Find the ones she uses.

Giving main ideas:	*Basically . . .* *The point / thing is . . .*
Adding ideas:	*Another thing is . . .*
Introducing a list:	*There are two problems. . . .* *. . . for two reasons.*
Ordinal numbers:	*First (of all), . . .* *Second (of all), / Secondly, . . .*
Numbers or letters:	*(Number) One, . . .* *Two, . . .* **or** *A, . . .* *B, . . .*

B *Pair work* Have a conversation about security cameras like the one above. Use these ideas or your own, and organize what you say. Take turns arguing for and against.

For security cameras
They help reduce crime rates.
They help the police solve crimes.
They make people feel safer.

Against security cameras
They're intrusive.
They're an invasion of privacy.
They're expensive. They're a waste of money.

A   *Do you think there should be security cameras everywhere?*
B   *Well, basically I think it's a good idea to have them. I mean, for two reasons. First, . . .*

SELF-STUDY
AUDIO CD
CD-ROM

2 Strategy plus *That's a good point.*

You can use **That's a good point** and other expressions like these to show someone has a valid argument – even if you don't completely agree:

That's true.
You've got a point (there).
I never (really) thought of it that way.

They help the police.

That's true.

▶ **In conversation . . .**

That's true is the second most common expression with **That's**, after **That's right**.

A Write a response to these points of view, using one of the expressions above and adding a different or an opposing view.

1. People who speed should lose their licenses, I think. Speeding causes so many accidents.
   That's true, but I think they should also be made to take more driving lessons.
2. I think they should use metal detectors in all public buildings. That way people wouldn't carry knives with them.
3. They should punish the parents of kids who skip school. It's the parents who should be responsible.
4. I don't think people should have to carry ID cards. I mean, what are you supposed to do if you go to the beach?
5. They should raise the legal age for driving to 20. There would be fewer accidents.

B *Pair work* Take turns presenting the views above and the other views that you wrote. Continue your arguments.

3 Listening and speaking *Different points of view*

A Listen to the class debate. Answer the questions.

1. Which of these topics is the class discussing? Check (✓) the topic.

   ☐ Raising the age limit to get married   ☐ Banning cars from city areas
   ☐ Sending dangerous drivers to prison   ☐ Raising the legal age for driving

2. What two arguments are given in favor of changing the law? Take notes.
3. What two arguments are given against changing the law? Take notes.

About you ▶ **B** Listen to these opinions from the debate again. Prepare a response to each point of view. Use an expression from the box, and add your own opinion.

1. _____
2. _____
3. _____
4. _____
5. _____

Useful expressions

That's a good point, but . . .
Absolutely! I agree with that.
Maybe, but on the other hand, . . .
That's a good idea.
I'm not sure about that for two reasons.

C *Group work* Discuss one of the topics in part A, item 1. Do you share the same views?

1 Reading

A Do you or any of your friends have a cam phone? What can you use a cam phone for? Are there any places where you're not allowed to use one? Why?

B Read the article. What is it about? Choose one of the ideas.

a. People using cell phones at work
b. People taking pictures for the wrong reasons
c. The advantages of cam phones

CAM PHONES, GO HOME!

by Carolina A. Miranda

Those camera-equipped cell phones may be the latest must-have tech product, with more than 31 million sold in North America last year alone. But the ability of users to snap pictures on the sly almost anywhere they go – and even put images on the Internet – has prompted a growing number of places to institute a ban on the devices.

Several large companies – even one of the leading producers of the phones – are among the companies that have prohibited employees from taking cam phones into sensitive research and production facilities, to prevent corporate espionage. Schools are banning them to halt cheating, since students have been nabbed shooting test questions and e-mailing them to others. Many courthouses ban the phones to prevent witness or juror intimidation. (At a superior court hearing, a witness was photographed by a cam-phone user who threatened to post the photo on the Web.) Most gyms have set limits, especially in locker rooms, fearing members could take pictures of people in various states of undress.

Those localized bans, however, do little for anyone in a public area. One popular Web site proudly touts photos shot by cam phones in malls and parking lots. "People need to be aware that whatever you do in a public space can be recorded," says attorney Kevin Bankston of the Electronic Frontier Foundation, an online civil-liberties group.

Source: © 2005 Time Inc. All rights reserved. Reprinted from Time Magazine with permission.

C Find expressions in the article to complete the sentences below.

1. Everyone wants a cam phone. They've become a ___must-have___ tech product.
2. With a cam phone, you can take pictures _____ – without anyone knowing.
3. There are sometimes spies in a company that use cam phones for _____ .
4. Criminals sometimes scare or threaten jurors or witnesses. That's called _____ .
5. Cam phones are often banned in specific locations, but these _____ don't protect people in public places.
6. One Web site boldly advertises cam-phone photos. They _____ the photos proudly.
7. There's a _____ group that helps protect people's privacy and freedom online.

D Find these verbs in the article. Can you guess their meaning from context?

snap	**institute**	**prevent**	**nabbed**
prompted	**prohibited**	**halt**	**shooting**

E Read the article again, and find . . .

1. what happens to many of the photographs that people take with cam phones.
2. four places that have banned cam phones and why.
3. why people need to be careful about what they do in public.

2 *Speaking and writing* *Letters to the editor . . .*

A *Pair work* What do you think about the magazine article on page 50? Discuss the questions.

1. Do you think the topic of the article is relevant?
2. Are you concerned about the issues it raises?
3. Have you ever seen anyone use a cam phone inappropriately?
4. What should be done to prevent people from misusing cam phones?

B Write a letter to the editor of the magazine, responding to the article. Use the ideas from your discussion above to state your views.

⊝⊝⊝ Document 1 ⊝
A letter to the editor . . .
I was interested to read your recent article on cam phones. I think the problems it talked about are very relevant here, **as** so many people now use them.
I think the biggest problem is cheating in schools, **since** students can use their phones to take photos of test questions and then send them to other students.
I have never used a cam phone, **because** I would rather use my digital camera to take photos.

Help note

Giving reasons

- You can use *because*, *since*, and *as* to give reasons.
  Cam phones should be banned in schools, because / since / as they can be misused by students.

- You can use *because* in all cases. Use *since* only to give reasons that the reader already knows or can guess. *As* is more formal.

C Post your letters around the classroom. Read your classmates' letters. Find someone who raises an issue you hadn't thought about.

3 *Free talk* *Lawmakers*

See *Free talk 5* for more speaking practice.

Vocabulary notebook

It's a crime!

Learning tip Word charts

One way to write down new words is to use word charts. You can group related ideas together, which will help you learn and remember them.

1 Complete the word chart about crime using the words and expressions in the box.

| burglar | murderer | steals from stores | paints on public buildings |
| murder | shoplifting | vandalism | breaks into a building to steal |

Crime	Criminal	Activity
burglary		
	vandal	
		kills or murders people
	shoplifter	

2 Word builder Find out the meaning of the crime words in this chart. Then complete the chart, adding more words and definitions.

Crime	Criminal	Activity
arson		
blackmail		
hijacking		
joyriding		
mugging		

On your own

Look through an English-language newspaper, and highlight all the words that are connected with crime and law. How many of them do you already know?

Strange events

In Unit 6, you learn how to . . .

- use the past perfect.
- use responses with *So* and *Neither*.
- talk about coincidences, superstitions, and strange events.
- repeat your ideas to make your meaning clear.
- use *just* to make what you say stronger or softer.

2

When you can tell what someone else is thinking, you are experiencing _____ .

1

When you have the strange feeling that you have been somewhere or experienced something before, you are having _____ .

4

When you unexpectedly run into someone you know – for example, in another city – you call it _____ .

3

When you see an unexplained object in the sky, you might be seeing _____ .

Before you begin . . .

Complete the sentences with the words below.

- telepathy
- a coincidence
- déjà vu
- a UFO (unidentified flying object)

Have you ever had an experience like these?
Do you know anyone else who has?

Have you ever experienced an *amazing coincidence?*

It's Gerry!

SPENCER COLLEGE

> Actually, yeah. One thing that sticks in my mind is . . . years ago, I was out in the Australian outback, driving through the desert. One night, I had set up camp and was cooking, and this van appeared out of nowhere with two guys in it. It was nice to have company because I hadn't spoken to anyone in days – I'd gone on this trip by myself, you see. Well, it turned out one of them had graduated from the same college I did. Small world, huh?
>
> **– Glen Hutt**

> Oh, yeah, I think life is full of coincidences. I remember one time – I had just met my husband-to-be, and we hadn't known each other long. Well, he was showing me photos of an old friend that he hadn't seen or spoken to in years, a college friend who'd moved to Spain. Gerry. Anyway, there we were, looking at these photos when the phone rang, and – you'll never believe it – it was his friend Gerry! He just called out of the blue.
>
> **– Emma Rivers**

1 Getting started

A 🖸 Listen. What coincidences did these people experience?

Figure it out

B Complete the answers. Look at the anecdotes to help you.

1. Why was Glen happy to have company?   Because he _____ to anyone in days.
2. Why wasn't Glen with his friends?   Because he _____ on the trip by himself.
3. Were Emma's husband and Gerry close?   Yes, but they _____ to each other in years.
4. What did Emma find out about Gerry?   He _____ to Spain years ago.

2 Grammar *The past perfect* 💿

> **Use the past perfect to talk about things that happened before an event in the past.**
> I **had set up** camp and was cooking, and this van appeared out of nowhere.
> I **had** just **met** my husband-to-be, and he was showing me photos . . . when the phone rang.
>
> **The past perfect is often used to give explanations or reasons why things happened.**
> It was nice to have company because I **hadn't spoken** to anyone in days.
> Gerry was a college friend that he **hadn't seen** in years. He**'d moved** to Spain.
>
> **Questions and short answers in the past perfect**
> **Had** you **gone** by yourself?   **Had** they **been** in touch?   Where **had** he **moved to**?
>   Yes, I had.   No, they hadn't.   To Spain.

A Complete the stories with either the simple past or past perfect. Sometimes both are possible. Then practice with a partner.

1. *A* Have you ever been talking about someone, and then they called you?
   B Yeah. That happens to me a lot. In fact, last week I was thinking about a friend who I _____ (not call) in ages. I think I _____ (throw away) his phone number by accident, and we _____ (not be) in touch for months. Anyway, he _____ (call) me out of the blue. It turned out that he _____ (lose) my number, too, but then he _____ (find) it.

2. *A* Have you ever run into someone you were thinking about?
   B No, I haven't, but I've experienced other coincidences. For example, one time a friend of mine _____ (call) me because she _____ (leave) her purse on the subway. She _____ (not know) what to do. And right then, my sister _____ (come) home with a purse that she _____ (find) on the subway, and guess what? It _____ (be) my friend's purse!

3. *A* Have you ever met anyone with the same birthday as you?
   B Yes, my friend Tom. The funny thing is, last year I _____ (decide) to buy him something special because he _____ (help) me fix my car many times. So I _____ (get) him this camera that we _____ (see) when we were out shopping the week before. When we _____ (open) our presents, we _____ (laugh). We _____ (buy) each other exactly the same thing!

About you → **B** *Pair work* Ask and answer the questions. Tell your own stories.

3 Listening *It's a small world!*

💿 Listen to Jody tell a friend about a coincidence. Answer the questions.

1. How did Jody and Janeen first get to know each other?
2. How long have they been friends now?
3. How long had they been out of touch when they met up again?
4. Where did they both end up living?
5. How did they try to get in touch again?
6. What coincidence makes both speakers say "small world"?

SUPERSTITIONS FROM AROUND THE WORLD

Taiwan If you see a crow in the morning, you will have a bad day.

South Korea If you give a boyfriend or girlfriend a pair of shoes, he or she will leave you.

Japan It's lucky to find a tea leaf floating upright in a cup of green tea.

Argentina Pick up any coins you find, and you'll soon come into money.

Thailand Dream of a snake holding you tightly, and you will soon meet your soul mate.

Peru If you put clothes on inside out, you will get a nice surprise.

Brazil If you leave your purse on the floor, your money will disappear.

Mexico If a bride wears pearls, she will cry all her married life.

Venezuela If someone sweeps over an unmarried woman's feet with a broom, she'll never get married.

Turkey Your wish will come true if you stand between two people with the same name.

1 Building vocabulary

A Read the superstitions above. How many have you heard of? Do you have any similar superstitions in your country?

Word sort → **B** Complete the chart with the superstitions above. Add ideas. Then compare with a partner.

It's good luck to . . .	It's bad luck to . . .
find a green tea leaf floating upright.	leave your purse on the floor.

2 Speaking and listening *Lucky or not?*

A Do you know any superstitions about the things below? Tell the class.

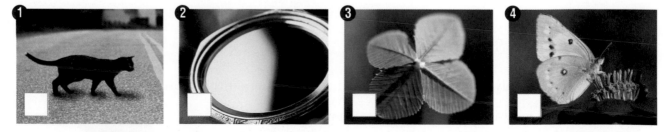

B 💿 Listen to four people talk about superstitions. Do they think the things above are lucky (**L**) or unlucky (**U**)? Write *L* or *U* in the boxes.

C 💿 Listen again. Can you write down each superstition? Compare with a partner.

3 Building language

A  Listen. Is Angie superstitious? How about Terry? Practice the conversation.

Angie Gosh, this looks good. I'm so hungry.

Terry So am I. Could you pass the salt?

Angie Sure. . . . Whoops! You know, it's supposed to be
unlucky to spill salt.

Terry It is? I didn't know that.

Angie No, neither did I, until I read it on the Internet.

Terry Actually, I don't believe in all that superstitious stuff.

Angie Oh, I do. Now I always throw a pinch of salt over my
shoulder if I spill it. And I never put shoes on the table.

Terry Well, neither do I. But that's because they're dirty.

Angie And I always walk around a ladder – never under it.

Terry Oh, so do I. But that's so nothing falls on my head!

Figure it out

B Underline two expressions above that mean *Me neither*, and two that mean *Me too*.

4 Grammar *Responses with* **So** *and* **Neither**

I'm hungry.	I'm **not** very superstitious.
So am I. (I am too.)	**Neither am** I. (I'm not either.)
I always **walk** around ladders.	I **didn't know** it was unlucky to spill salt.
So do I. (I do too.)	**Neither did** I. (I didn't either.)

A Respond to each of these statements with *So* or
Neither. Then practice with a partner.

1. I think it's silly to be superstitious.   So do I.
2. I don't know anyone who is superstitious.
3. I didn't know the superstition about spilling salt.
4. I walk under ladders all the time.
5. I'm usually a very lucky person.
6. I've never found a four-leaf clover.

> **In conversation . . .**
>
> Responses in the present tense are the most common.
>
> So / Neither do I.
> So / Neither am I.
> So / Neither did I.
> So / Neither have I.
> So / Neither was I.

About you

B *Pair work* Take turns making the sentences true for you and giving true responses.

"I don't think it's silly to be superstitious."   *"Neither do I."* **or** *"Actually, I think it is a bit silly."*

C *Group work* Do you believe in any superstitions? Tell the group. Are there any that
you all have in common?

"I always make a wish when there's a full moon."   *"So do I, if I remember."*

5 Vocabulary notebook *Keep your fingers crossed.*

See page 62 for a useful way to log and learn vocabulary.

1 Conversation strategy *Making your meaning clear*

A How many different ways does this person say his friend is odd? Find the words he uses.

"One of my friends is kind of odd. I mean, she's nice and everything, but she's just a bit weird sometimes. You know, she says some strange things, so people think she's kind of funny."

Now listen to Carlos and Nicole. What does Nicole say about her dreams?

Carlos	**You look tired. Are you OK?**
Nicole	**Yeah, I'm fine. I guess I just had a bad night. I often don't sleep too well. You know, I have some strange dreams.**
Carlos	**You do? I hardly ever dream.**
Nicole	**Yeah. I, um . . . I've had some weird dreams. Really weird dreams. And they're scary. They're always scary ones. They're never good ones. They're just weird and off the wall.**
Carlos	**Like nightmares?**
Nicole	**Yeah. I have really bad nightmares. And I tend to have dreams that come true every once in a while. I try to be careful. You know the saying, "Don't tell a bad dream before breakfast because it might come true"?**
Carlos	**Never heard that. So, you tell it after breakfast?**
Nicole	**Yeah. Or sometimes not at all.**

Notice how Nicole repeats her ideas to make her meaning clear. Sometimes she repeats the same words, and sometimes she uses different words. Find examples in the conversation.

"I've had some weird dreams. Really weird dreams."

"They're always scary ones. They're never good ones."

B Complete each sentence by using a word from the list to repeat the main idea. Then discuss the statements with a partner. Do you agree with them?

1. Nightmares can be very scary, you know. They can be really _____ .
2. I think other people's dreams are really interesting. Really _____ .
3. Dreams have no meaning. They're just weird, _____ thoughts.
4. Insomnia must be awful. I mean, not being able to sleep must be _____ .
5. Most kids are afraid of the dark at some point. They all get _____ .
6. Sleepwalking is pretty common. It's nothing _____ .

crazy
fascinating
frightening
scared
terrible
unusual

SELF-STUDY
AUDIO CD
CD-ROM

2 Strategy plus *just*

You can use **just** to make what you say stronger.

My dreams are just weird.

I guess I just had a bad night.

You can also use **just** to make what you say softer.

▶ **In conversation . . .**

Just is one of the top 30 words. Over half of its uses are to make ideas stronger or softer.

A 💿 Listen. Are these people using *just* to make what they say stronger or softer? Check (✓) the boxes.

	Stronger	Softer
1. I often think about people, and then they call me. It's just amazing.	☐	☐
2. I just love all those TV shows about telepathy. They're fascinating.	☐	☐
3. I don't believe people can read minds. I just think they make good guesses.	☐	☐
4. I believe you can make wishes come true. You just have to try.	☐	☐
5. I don't think it's possible to hypnotize people. I just don't believe you can.	☐	☐
6. I don't think people who believe in UFOs are crazy. I think they just have active imaginations.	☐	☐

About you → **B** *Pair work* Are any of the sentences true for you? Tell a partner.

"I often think about people, and then I see them or they call. But I think it's just a coincidence."

3 Speaking naturally *Stressing new information*

Nicole *I have some strange **dreams**. . . . some **weird** dreams. **Really** weird dreams. And they're **scary**. They're **always** scary.*

A 💿 Listen and repeat what Nicole says about her dreams. Notice how the new information in each sentence gets the strongest stress.

B 💿 Can you predict which words have the strongest stress in the conversation below? Underline one word in each sentence. Then listen and check. Practice the conversation with a partner, and use your own information.

A Do you ever have bad <u>dreams</u>?
B You mean scary dreams? Like nightmares?
A Yeah. Dreams that make you all upset.
B No. I usually have nice dreams. Fun dreams. What about you?
A Oh, I never dream. At least, I never remember my dreams.

1 Reading

A Have you ever known any identical twins? How were they alike? Tell the class.

B Read the title of the article and the summary. What's the story about? Predict two things you think will happen in the story.

Separated **at birth...** by J.D. Heyman

Tamara Rabi and Adriana Scott

Growing up, they had a weird feeling something was missing. Turned out that "something" was their long-lost twin. After constantly mistaking one for the other, friends put two and two together and arranged a reunion.

Within weeks of showing up for her freshman year at Long Island's Hofstra University in New York, strange things started happening to Tamara Rabi. Strangers would smile and wave at her, then walk away peeved when she told them she didn't know them. "They must have thought I was crazy," says Rabi, 20. "Sometimes they'd ask me, 'Do you have a twin sister?' And I'd say 'No.'"

Just down the road at Adelphi University, Adriana Scott kept hearing similar questions about her dead ringer* at Hofstra. Nudged by friends, the young women got in touch by e-mail and discovered they both had been born in Guadalajara, Mexico, and adopted. Then Adriana's mother, Diana Scott, dropped a bombshell: When she and her late husband Peter, a vice president at a moving company, adopted her, they knew she had a twin who at the time was unavailable for adoption. Adriana's discovery "was a moment I'd dreaded for 20 years," says Diana, a receptionist.

While the Scotts raised Adriana in the Long Island suburbs, Tamara's adoptive parents, Yitzhak and Judy Rabi, who didn't know she was a twin, brought her up in Manhattan. "My family was very cautious," says Tamara, who learned about Adriana shortly after Yitzhak had died at age 58. "Even after they saw her photo, they had doubts. I was, like, 'C'mon, guys, the picture looks exactly like me!'"

Late last year, the girls agreed to meet on neutral ground at a local McDonald's and discovered that practically the only noticeable difference between them was a small birthmark above Tamara's right eyebrow. "Her voice was what got me," says Adriana. "I just sat there in shock." Even their mothers had trouble telling them apart.

Since then, the reunited twins and their widowed moms have formed a close bond, and recently they took a spa vacation together at a plush resort. "Tamara's sister could have been anyone in the world, but it turned out to be this wonderful girl," says Judy, 56. Adds Tamara: "It's like I'm starting a whole new life. For 20 years I haven't had a sister, and now I do."

*dead ringer someone who looks identical to someone else
Source: *People* magazine

C Now read the article. Answer the questions. Were your predictions correct?

1. How did Tamara and Adriana get to know each other?
2. How are Tamara and Adriana alike? How are they different?
3. Have you ever heard of a story similar to theirs?

D *Pair work* Find these words and expressions in the article. Can you figure out their meaning from the context? Match each expression with a similar expression on the right.

1. put two and two together ____
2. showing up ____
3. peeved ____
4. nudged ____
5. dropped a bombshell ____
6. dreaded ____
7. on neutral ground ____
8. telling them apart ____
9. formed a close bond ____

a. annoyed
b. arriving
c. developed a good relationship
d. knowing who is who
e. encouraged
f. feared
g. figured something out
h. gave shocking news
i. at a place neither person knows well

2 Speaking and writing *Family stories*

About you →

A *Group work* Do you have any amazing stories to tell about your family? Discuss the questions.

- What's your family's background and history? Does your family have an interesting story?
- How did your parents meet? How about your grandparents?
- Is there anyone in your family you don't see very often? Why?
- Has your family ever had a family reunion? What was it like?
- Are you close to one particular member of your family? How did you become close?

B Choose one of the topics above, and write a story to share with the class.

Document 1

A true romance . . .

Before starting college, my mother had never ridden a bicycle in her life. Soon after arriving on campus, however, she met a guy who was the president of the college cycling club, and he invited her to join. My mother became a member of the club and bought a new bike.

The next weekend, she showed up at the group meeting with her new bicycle, and she was very surprised. She hadn't realized it was a racing club and that everyone had racing bikes. Her new bike was big and heavy, and it had a huge basket for shopping and books. She almost turned around and left after seeing all the professional-looking cyclists, but the club president persuaded her to stay. He rode with her – at the back.

To make a long story short, this guy ended up marrying my mother. He's my father, and he and my mother still love to go cycling together.

Help note

Prepositional time clauses

Notice in the sentences below, **she** is the subject of both verbs.

Before starting *college, she had never ridden a bicycle.* = "Before she started college, she had never ridden a bicycle."

Soon after arriving *on campus, she met a guy.* = "Soon after she arrived on campus, she met a guy."

*She almost left **after seeing** all the other cyclists.* = "She almost left after she saw the other cyclists."

C *Class activity* Read your classmates' stories. Which story interests you the most?

3 Free talk *Can you believe it?*

See *Free talk 6* for more speaking practice.

Keep your fingers crossed.

Learning tip *Grouping vocabulary*

A good way to learn sayings, like proverbs or superstitions, is to group them according to topics, using word webs.

> **Good luck!**
>
> Over 50% of the uses of the word **luck** are when people talk about or wish others **Good luck!**
>
> Less than 5% of its uses are to talk about **dumb**, **bad**, **poor**, **tough**, or **rotten luck**.

1 For each topic below, find a superstition from this unit. Write the ones you want to remember.

Dream of a snake, and you'll find your soul mate.

(love)

It's good luck to find a four-leaf clover.

(good luck)

(money)

If you pick up coins, you'll come into money.

(bad luck)

If you break a mirror, you'll have seven years of bad luck.

2 ***Word builder*** Can you complete these superstitions? If you don't know them, you can look up the phrases in quotation marks (" ") in a search engine on the Internet. Then add them to the word webs above.

Finding a ladybug . . .
If you open an umbrella indoors, . . .
Cut your nails on Friday, . . .

Bringing a new broom into a new house . . .
Putting clothes on with your left arm first . . .
Leave a house by the same door . . .

On your own

Ask 5 people if they are superstitious about anything. Translate their superstitions into English.

1 What are you supposed to do?

What do these signs mean? Write one or two sentences for each sign using *supposed to* or *not supposed to*. Compare with a partner. Where might you see these signs?

A **This one means you're not supposed to use your cell phone. You're supposed to turn it off.**

B **Yeah. You're supposed to turn cell phones off in hospitals, I think. And on planes.**

2 You can say that again!

A Can you complete the second sentence so that it repeats the main idea of the first sentence? Add *just* to make the meaning stronger or softer. Compare with a partner.

1. I really enjoy going to parties. I _just love going to parties_ .
2. I sometimes get a bit nervous when I meet new people. I _____ .
3. I don't go out every night because it's too expensive. It _____ .
4. I'm never on time when I have to meet friends. I _____ .

B Make the sentences true for you. Tell a partner your sentences. Use statement questions to check that you understand your partner's sentences.

A **I really don't enjoy going to parties. I just hate being with a lot of people.**

B **Really? So you prefer to stay home?**

3 Crime doesn't pay.

A How many ways can you complete the sentences below? Make true sentences.

	Crime		Punishment	Criminals		Punishment
People who are convicted of	shoplifting	usually get	fined.	I think shoplifters	should be	fined.

B *Pair work* Organize and explain your views. Say when your partner makes a good point.

A **People who are convicted of shoplifting usually get fined. I think shoplifters should be fined. First, because it's not a really serious crime, and second, . . .**

B **That's a good point. But I think sometimes shoplifters should be sent to jail. For repeat offenses, or when they steal something really expensive.**

4 A weird week

A Read the story and answer the questions below. Use the past perfect in your answers.

Last week, Eric had some bad luck and some good luck. Monday was a bad day. First, he saw a crow on his car when he left for work. After work, he went shopping with his girlfriend. She spent all her money on an expensive sweater, so he had to buy them both dinner. In the restaurant, Eric yelled at her for spending so much money, and she got very angry. On Tuesday, Eric bought her a gift to apologize – some sneakers – but she was still mad, and on Wednesday, she broke up with him.

On Thursday, Eric had a strange dream about a snake winding itself tightly around his leg. He didn't sleep well and overslept on Friday morning. He got dressed in a hurry and accidentally put his sweater on inside out. Later, while he was waiting in line at the bank, a woman behind him said, "Excuse me. Your sweater is inside out." He turned around and realized she was his old college friend, Sarah. He hadn't seen her since their graduation six years ago. What a nice surprise! Eric remembered his dream and suddenly thought, "This is the woman I'm going to marry."

1. Why did Eric have to pay for his girlfriend's dinner?
2. Why did Eric want to apologize?
3. Why did he oversleep on Friday morning?
4. Why was his sweater inside out?
5. Why was it a surprise to see Sarah?
6. Why did Eric have that last thought?

"Eric had to pay for his girlfriend's dinner because she had spent all her money on a sweater."

B *Pair work* Look at the superstitions on page 56. How might a superstitious person explain the events in the story? How many superstitions can you use? Discuss your ideas.

"Maybe Eric had a bad day on Monday because he'd seen a crow in the morning."

5 Get this!

Fill in the blanks with the correct forms of the *get* expressions in the box. Then practice.

get around to	get over	get through
✓get it	get the feeling	get used to

Ann My sister and her boyfriend just broke up. She's so upset.
Bill I don't ___get it___ . They were the perfect couple.
Ann I _____ that she was expecting it. She'll _____ it soon.
Bill Did they ever get engaged? Or didn't they _____ it?
Ann They did, but she'll soon _____ being single again.
Bill It's a tough time, but she'll _____ it.

Self-check
How sure are you about these areas? Circle the percentages.

grammar
20% 40% 60% 80% 100%
vocabulary
20% 40% 60% 80% 100%
conversation strategies
20% 40% 60% 80% 100%

· ·

Study plan
What do you want to review? Circle the lessons.

grammar
4A 4B 5A 5B 6A 6B
vocabulary
4A 4B 5A 5B 6A 6B
conversation strategies
4C 5C 6C

6 Things in common?

Complete the sentences and compare with a partner. Say if you are the same or different. If you are the same, use *So* or *Neither*.

I believe in . . .   I don't believe in . . .   I was going to . . .
Once I tried . . .   I'm not a fan of . . .   I'm not supposed to . . .

"I believe in UFOs." "So do I. I think I saw one once."

Problem solving

In Unit 7, you learn how to . . .

- use causative *get* and *have* to talk about getting things done.
- use *need* + passive infinitive and *need* + verb + *-ing*.
- talk about errands, things that need to be fixed, and solving problems.
- speak informally in "shorter sentences."
- use expressions like *Uh-oh*, *Ouch*, and *Oops* when things go wrong.

1	a camera store
2	a copy shop
3	the optometrist

4	the dry cleaner's
5	a garage
6	a hair salon / a barbershop

Before you begin . . .
Where do you go when . . .

- you need a haircut?
- you need new glasses?
- you need some photocopies?

- there's a big stain on your jacket?
- you need a memory card for your camera?
- your car or motorbike breaks down?

Do it yourself!

We asked people what jobs they do themselves in order to save money. Here's what they said:

Have you ever cut your own hair to save money?

"I have, actually. But it looked so bad that I went to the most expensive place in town and had a hairdresser cut it again. I'll never try that again! Now I always get it cut professionally at a good hair salon, though I get a friend to cut my bangs occasionally. That saves me some money."

— Min Sook Kim
Seoul, South Korea

Do you do your own car repairs?

"Well, I can do routine things like put oil in the car. But, to be honest, I get my brother to fix most things. And if there's something seriously wrong with my car, I have my uncle take a look at it at his garage. I can get it fixed there pretty cheaply. I also have it serviced there once a year."

— Marcus Aldóvar
Bogotá, Colombia

Do you do your own home decorating?

"My wife and I are having a new house built right now, but we're going to do all the painting and decorating ourselves. We've done it before. My sister's an interior designer, so we'll have her choose the colors and get her to pick out curtains, too. She's got great taste."

— Martin and Jill Snow
Calgary, Canada

Do you ever do your own repairs around the house?

"Not anymore! Once I tried fixing the dishwasher myself because I didn't want to pay to have someone come and repair it. But I didn't realize I had to turn off the water first. So I fixed the problem, but I flooded the entire apartment! And it cost a fortune to have the water damage repaired."

— Bella Clark
Miami, U.S.A.

1 Getting started

A 🔘 Listen. Which jobs have these people done themselves? Were they successful?

Figure it out **B** Which sentences are true about the people above? Choose *a* or *b*.

1. a. Min Sook always cuts her own hair. b. Min Sook gets her hair cut at a salon.
2. a. Marcus always fixes his car himself. b. Marcus often gets his car fixed at a garage.
3. a. The Snows are going to paint their house. b. The Snows are going to have their house painted.
4. a. Bella repaired her dishwasher. b. Bella had her dishwasher repaired.

2 Grammar *Causative get and have* 💿

get + person + to + verb; have + person + verb	get / have + object + past participle
I **get** my brother **to fix** my car.	I **get** my car **fixed** at my uncle's garage.
We'll **get** my sister **to choose** colors for our house.	We're **having** a new house **built** now.
My hair looked bad, so I **had** a hairdresser **cut** it again.	I always **get** my hair **cut** professionally.
I didn't pay to **have** someone **repair** my dishwasher.	It cost a lot to **have** the water damage **repaired**.

About you → **A** Write answers to the following questions. Use the words in **bold** in your responses. Then ask and answer the questions with a partner.

1. Do you usually **get** your hair **cut** professionally? How often do you **get** it **cut**?
2. Have you ever **had** a friend **cut** your hair? How did it turn out?
3. Do you have a bicycle, motorcycle, or car? Where do you **get** it **fixed**?
4. If you had a flat tire, would you **get** someone **to change** it for you or do it yourself?
5. Do you take a lot of clothes to the dry cleaner's? Is it expensive to **get** things **cleaned**?
6. Do you iron your own clothes? Do you ever **get** someone **to iron** things for you?
7. Do you do your own painting at home, or do you **have** it **done** by a professional?
8. Do you ever **have** people **come** to the house to repair things? What do they repair?

B *Pair work* What things do you have done professionally? Where do you get these things done? Make a list and compare with your partner. Do you handle things the same way?

A I get my shirts cleaned at the dry cleaner's. What about you?
B I wash my own shirts, but I sometimes get my sister to iron them.

3 Listening *Wedding on a budget*

A 💿 Listen. Molly and Mark are talking about things they need to do to get ready for their wedding. What topics do they agree on? Check (✓) the boxes.

B 💿 Listen again. Which things are Molly and Mark going to have done professionally? Which things are they or their families going to do themselves? Make two lists.

What needs to be done?

1 Building language

A  Listen. What is Isaac good at fixing? Practice the conversation.

Anna Isaac, something's wrong with the shower. It won't turn off completely. It keeps dripping.

Isaac Yeah? Maybe the showerhead needs replacing.

Anna Oh, it's probably just a washer or something that needs to be replaced. Can you take a look at it?

Isaac Me? I'm not a plumber. I don't even know what's wrong with it.

Anna I know. But you're always so good when the TV needs to be fixed. You know, when the screen needs adjusting.

Isaac Yeah, well, that's an emergency!

> **Figure it out**

B Can you say *We need to replace the showerhead* in two different ways? Use the conversation to help you. Start like this.

"The showerhead needs . . ."

2 Grammar *need + passive infinitive and* **need** *+ verb + -ing*

need + passive infinitive	**need + verb + -ing**
The TV needs **to be fixed**.	The TV needs **fixing**.
The screen needs **to be adjusted**.	The screen needs **adjusting**.

The structure **need + verb + -ing** *occurs mainly with verbs like* changing, cleaning, adjusting, replacing, recharging, **etc.**

A Complete the statements below in two ways. Use *need* + passive infinitive and *need* + verb + *-ing*. Compare with a partner.

1. There's a problem with our car. The brakes _____ (adjust).
2. My computer's very slow. Maybe the memory _____ (upgrade).
3. I can't make any calls right now because my cell phone _____ (recharge).
4. My camera is always going dead. The batteries _____ (replace) constantly.
5. The closet light won't turn on. The bulb _____ (change or tighten).
6. Our air conditioner isn't working very well. Maybe the filter _____ (clean).

> **About you**

B Pair work Are any of the sentences true for you? Do you have any similar problems?

*A **I don't think there are any problems with my car. Well, one of the tail lights needs replacing.***

*B **My car needs to be serviced. I should get it done soon, actually.***

3 Building vocabulary

A Anna is pointing out more problems to Isaac. Can you guess what things she's talking about? Complete the sentences below. Then compare answers with a partner.

1. "The ___microwave___ isn't working. Nothing's happening. It **won't turn on**."
2. "The _____ is **leaking**. And there's a _____ in the door."
3. "The _____ **keeps flickering** on and off. And I **got a shock** from it."
4. "The _____ is **loose**. If it **falls off**, we won't be able to open the door."
5. "The ceiling _____ is **making a funny noise**."
6. "There are _____ all over the counter, and they're all **scratched**."
7. "That _____ is **torn**. And look – there's a big **hole** in the other one."
8. "There's a coffee **stain** on the _____."
9. "The _____ is a half hour **slow**. Actually, I think it **stopped**. The battery must be **dead**."

Word sort ⇒ **B** Can you think of two items for each of the problems below? Do you have any things like these that need to be fixed? Tell a partner.

Things that often . . .	Things that are often . . .	Things that often have . . .
leak: refrigerator, pen	scratched:	a dent in them:
fall off:	torn:	a stain on them:
make a funny noise:	loose:	a hole in them:

C Group work Make a "to do" list for Anna and Isaac, and prioritize each task. Guess what might be wrong with each thing in their kitchen. How can they get the problems fixed? Which things need to be done right away?

A *I wonder what's wrong with the microwave. Why isn't it working?*
B *I don't know, but it's plugged in. They need to get it fixed pretty quickly.*
   I think they should take it to a repair shop and have someone look at it.
C *Actually, I think it probably needs to be replaced.*

TO DO
1.
2.
3.

4 Vocabulary notebook *Damaged goods*

See page 74 for a new way to log and learn vocabulary.

1 Conversation strategy *Speaking in "shorter sentences"*

A What words have the speakers "left out" of this conversation?

> *A* Ready? Want to get something to eat?
> *B* Love to. Almost ready.

Now listen to Kayla and Hector. What are they trying to do? Are they successful?

Kayla	Hi, there. . . . Ooh! Want some help?
Hector	Sure. Just take that end. Got it?
Kayla	Yeah. Think so. Oops! Wait a second.
Hector	OK. . . . Ready? One, two, three, lift.
Kayla	Ooh, it's heavy! . . . Ow! Just broke a nail.
Hector	Ouch! You OK?
Kayla	Yeah. But hurry up!
Hector	There. Shoot! It's not straight.
Kayla	Want me to fix it? . . . Better?
Hector	Yeah, . . . up a bit on the left.
Kayla	There you go. Done.
Hector	Thanks. Like it?
Kayla	Love it. It looks good. Really good.
Hector	Want some coffee?
Kayla	No, thanks. Can't drink it. Got any soda?
Hector	Sure. . . . Uh-oh! Don't have any. Sorry.

Notice how Kayla and Hector speak in "shorter sentences." They leave out words like *I* or *you*, and verbs like *do*, *be*, and *have*. People often do this in informal conversations, especially when it's clear who or what they're talking about. Find more examples.

> "(Do you) Want some help?"
> "(Are you) Ready?"
> "(I) Just broke a nail."

B Rewrite the conversation with shorter sentences. Compare with a partner and practice.

A Do you need this screwdriver? Here it is.
B Thanks. I can't get this shelf off the wall.
A Do you want me to try getting it off for you?
B Yes, thanks. Are you sure you've got time?
A Yes. . . . OK. That's done. Do you need help with anything else?
B Thank you. No, there's nothing else. Would you like a drink?
A I'd love one. Have you got any green tea?

SELF-STUDY
AUDIO CD
CD-ROM

2 *Strategy plus* *Uh-oh!*

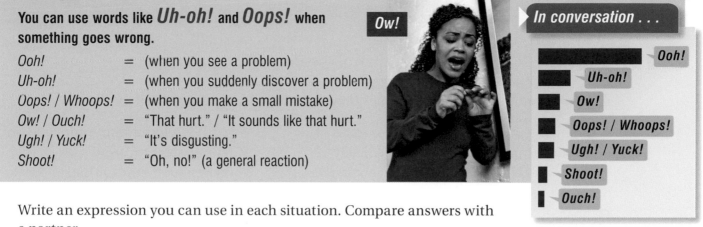

You can use words like **Uh-oh!** and **Oops!** when something goes wrong.

Ooh!	=	(when you see a problem)
Uh-oh!	=	(when you suddenly discover a problem)
Oops! / Whoops!	=	(when you make a small mistake)
Ow! / Ouch!	=	"That hurt." / "It sounds like that hurt."
Ugh! / Yuck!	=	"It's disgusting."
Shoot!	=	"Oh, no!" (a general reaction)

Ow!

In conversation . . .

Ooh!
Uh-oh!
Ow!
Oops! / Whoops!
Ugh! / Yuck!
Shoot!
Ouch!

Write an expression you can use in each situation. Compare answers with a partner.

1. You drop a hammer on your toe. __Ow!__
2. You miss a call on your cell phone. _____
3. You spill coffee on the table. _____
4. A friend tells you how she broke her arm. _____
5. You realized you just missed a class. _____
6. You put too much sugar in your coffee. _____

3 *Speaking naturally* *Short question and statement intonation*

Questions: Ready? OK? **Statements:** Ready. OK.

A Listen and repeat the words above. Notice the rising intonation for short questions and falling intonation for short statements.

B Listen. Is each sentence a question or a statement? Add a question mark (**?**) or a period (**.**) .

1. Better___
2. Got it___
3. Broke a nail___
4. Left a bit___
5. Done___
6. You need help

4 *Listening and speaking* *Fix it!*

A Listen. Which items are the people trying to fix? Number the pictures.

B Listen again. Do they solve the problems? Write *Yes* or *No* on the line.

C *Pair work* Choose one of the problems above. Role-play a conversation like the one on page 70.

1 Reading

A What's your problem-solving style? Do you do any of these things? Tell the class.

- Ignore the problem until the last minute.
- Do something – anything – immediately.
- Get as much information as you can first.

- Try different solutions until one works.
- Try one solution only.
- Take enough time to think of ideas.

B Read the article. Which of the ideas above are recommended?

Developing Your Problem-Solving Skills

by Janice Arenofsky

Problem solving is wrestling with algebra or chemistry homework. But it's also taking on the day-to-day challenges of being a human being. At school or work, you are confronted by challenging situations. For example, what do you do about a lost wallet, a misunderstanding with a friend or co-worker, or a forgotten assignment? How well and how quickly you deal with these situations matters. Your problem-solving skills can greatly influence your personal and professional success.

A+ Appeal

The ability to solve problems efficiently is one of the top 10 qualities that companies want in new employees. This is what Kellah M. Edens says. She is an education professor at the University of South Carolina in Columbia. "During job interviews, it's common to be asked 'what if' questions," says Edens. "How you answer will demonstrate your problem-solving ability. Generally, these questions deal with real problems in the workplace."

Why do interviewers ask "what if" questions? Applicants with good problem-solving skills usually have positive personality traits, such as patience, independence, and curiosity. Good problem solvers usually have self-esteem, competence, and a responsible attitude toward decision making. "Other problem-solving traits include flexibility, open-mindedness, and tolerance for ambiguity [uncertainty]," says Edens.

Step-by-Step

The most productive problem solvers are also creative. Take Albert Einstein. The world-famous physicist understood that most problems have many possible answers. And the first answer is not always the best. Generating multiple solutions is highly desirable. To do this, you must think less rigidly, or "outside the box," says Michael Michalko, author of *Thinkertoys: A Handbook of Business Creativity.*

Evaluate each alternative. Don't criticize yourself or feel embarrassed by any errors you make, writes Michael E. Martinez, an education professor at the University of California at Irvine. If one real-life exercise doesn't get the hoped-for result, try another and another. Remain coolheaded. "Allow enough time for ideas to form," suggests Edens.

How do you do that? Take a step-by-step approach to problem solving.

1. State the problem in the form of a question. Make it clear and specific.
2. Gather accurate information.
3. Brainstorm a wide variety of solutions, both creative and conventional.
4. Examine and try alternatives.
5. Choose a solution.

Source: *Weekly Reader*

C Find the underlined words in the article. Match each one with the best meaning below. Write the letter.

1. One type of problem solving is <u>wrestling with</u> difficult math homework. _____
2. Your problem-solving skills can <u>influence</u> your personal development. _____
3. The ability to solve problems <u>efficiently</u> is a quality that companies want. _____
4. Answering "what if" questions can <u>demonstrate</u> your problem-solving ability. _____
5. One problem-solving trait is <u>tolerance for</u> uncertainty. _____

a. the ability to live with   c. show   e. quickly and well
b. trying to solve   d. have an effect on

D Read the article again. Answer the questions.

1. Why is it important to develop problem-solving skills?
2. Why might employers ask "what if" questions during a job interview?
3. What traits do good problem solvers have? Why are they important?
4. How do you think Albert Einstein tried to solve problems? Why?
5. What must you do to generate multiple solutions? What two things *shouldn't* you do?

2 Speaking and writing *A good solution*

A *Group work* Consider the following problem. Discuss your ideas and agree on a solution. Use the five steps described in the article on page 72.

> *The students in your school do not have a place to study, or to meet and relax before or after class. The school building has an extra room, but it is old and dirty, and it does not have any furniture or equipment, such as chairs, tables, or a vending machine. Although the school has a limited budget, you would like to turn this space into a student lounge.*

B Write a proposal persuading the school to agree to your ideas. Describe the problem and how you plan to solve it.

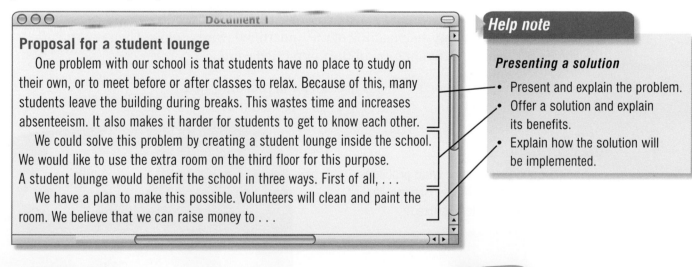

Document 1

Proposal for a student lounge

   One problem with our school is that students have no place to study on their own, or to meet before or after classes to relax. Because of this, many students leave the building during breaks. This wastes time and increases absenteeism. It also makes it harder for students to get to know each other.

   We could solve this problem by creating a student lounge inside the school. We would like to use the extra room on the third floor for this purpose. A student lounge would benefit the school in three ways. First of all, . . .

   We have a plan to make this possible. Volunteers will clean and paint the room. We believe that we can raise money to . . .

Help note

Presenting a solution

- Present and explain the problem.
- Offer a solution and explain its benefits.
- Explain how the solution will be implemented.

3 Free talk *What's the solution?*

See *Free talk 7* at the back of the book for more speaking practice.

Damaged goods

Learning tip Different forms of the same word

When you learn a new word, find out what type of word it is – a verb, a noun, an adjective, etc. – and whether it has a different form that can express the same idea.

There's a <u>leak</u> in the bathroom. (noun)	There's a <u>scratch</u> on this DVD. (noun)
The pipe is <u>leaking</u>. (verb)	This DVD is <u>scratched</u>. (adjective)

1 What's wrong with Mark's things? Complete the two sentences for each problem. Use the words in the box.

dent / dented	leak / leaking	scratch / scratched	stain / stained	tear / torn

1. There's a big _____ in the wheel of Mark's mountain bike. It's _____ .

2. There's a dark _____ on his T-shirt. It's _____ .

3. His shorts are _____ . There's a _____ in them.

4. His sunglasses are _____ . They have a _____ on them.

5. There's a _____ in his water bottle. It's _____ .

2 *Word builder* Find out the meaning of the underlined words below. Then rewrite the sentences using a different form of the underlined word.

1. My coffee mug is <u>chipped</u>.
2. The mirror is <u>cracked</u>.
3. There's a lot of <u>rust</u> on my car.
4. There's a lot of <u>mold</u> in my shower.

On your own

Look around your home. What problems are there? Label each one. Remove the label when the problem is fixed!

Lightbulb needs changing.

Behavior

In Unit 8, you learn how to . . .

■ use *would have*, *should have*, and *could have* to talk hypothetically about the past.

■ use *must have*, *may have*, *might have*, and *could have* to speculate about the past.

■ talk about your reactions and behavior in different situations.

■ describe people's emotions and personal qualities.

■ use expressions such as *That reminds me (of)* to share experiences.

■ use *like* informally in conversation.

Before you begin . . .

Can you think of any situations that would make you . . .

■ hug someone?   ■ lose your temper?

■ laugh out loud?   ■ hang up on someone?

■ sulk? mope?   ■ yell at someone?

Last night this guy called, trying to sell me a magazine subscription. Normally, I would have been more polite – you know, I would have just said no and then hung up. But he was the fourth caller, and it was after 10:00. So I just lost it. I yelled at him for several minutes, and I finally hung up on him. At that point, I couldn't have done much else, I don't think, because I was too mad. I know I shouldn't have lost my temper – he was just doing his job – but, I mean, what would you have done? I suppose I could have apologized. Or, I could have asked him to put me on their "do not call" list. Actually, that's what I should have done. I'll do that next time!

1 Getting started

A Listen to Olivia tell her friends about a phone call she got last night. What made Olivia lose her temper? How did she behave towards the caller?

Figure it out

B What can you say about Olivia's behavior? Can you imagine your own behavior in the same situation? Complete the sentences and compare with a partner.

1. She should have _____ .
2. She shouldn't have _____ .
3. I would have _____ .
4. I wouldn't have _____ .

2 Speaking naturally Reduction of *have* in past modals

Olivia should **have** been more polite. (should've)	I would **have** said no and hung up. (would've)
She shouldn't **have** lost her temper. (shouldn't've)	I wouldn't **have** yelled at him. (wouldn't've)
She could **have** apologized. (could've)	I wouldn't **have** hung up on him. (wouldn't've)

A Listen and repeat the sentences above. Notice the reduction of *have*.

About you

B *Pair work* Which sentences do you agree with? Tell a partner.

"I would have said no and hung up."   *"Me too. I wouldn't have yelled at him."*

3 Grammar *Past modals would have, should have, could have*

You can use these past modals to talk hypothetically about the past.

Imagine your *behavior in a* *situation:*	What **would** you **have done**? I **would have said** no politely. I **wouldn't have lost** my temper.	**Would** you **have gotten** mad? Yes, I probably **would have**.
Say what was *the right thing* *to do:*	What **should** she **have done**? She **should have said** no politely. She **shouldn't have yelled** at him.	**Should** she **have yelled** at him? No, she really **shouldn't have**.
Say what other *possibilities* *there were:*	What else **could** she **have done**? She **could have told** him not to call again. She **couldn't have done** much else.	**Could** she **have been** more polite? I feel she **could have**.

▶ **In conversation . . .**

I would is 20 times more common than *I'd* with past modals.

A Think about these situations, and answer each question. Write as many ideas as you can.

1. Tom's co-workers hid his laptop as a joke. Tom lost his temper and then sulked all day. Would you have reacted like Tom? What should he have done?
   I wouldn't have sulked. I would have . . .
   Tom should have laughed about it and . . .

2. Andrea's boyfriend called to cancel their date at the last minute. She told him she didn't want to see him again and then hung up on him. Should she have done that? What would you have done?

3. Joshua's neighbors were making too much noise late one night. He opened the window and yelled at them. Was that the right thing to do? What else could he have done?

4. Nathan's parents disapproved of one of his friends, so he got angry and yelled, "You are so narrow-minded!" What do you think of his reaction? What else could he have said?

5. Katy saw someone in a parked car throw litter out of the window. She picked it up and threw it right back into the car. Should she have done that? What would you have done?

B *Pair work* Compare your answers. Do you agree? What other possible solutions can you think of?

About *you*
C *Group work* Take turns telling true stories about the situations below. Listen to your classmates, and make suggestions. How should they have reacted? What could they have done differently?

Think about the last time you . . .

- had an argument.
- made a complaint.
- sulked or moped.
- lost your temper.
- yelled at someone.
- hung up on someone.

1 Building vocabulary

A Read the article below. In general, do you agree or disagree with these statements? Check (✓) the boxes.

EMOTIONAL INTELLIGENCE

*Emotional **intelligence*** is the ability to manage your own and other people's emotions. Emotionally **intelligent** people can express their feelings clearly and appropriately, and they are generally optimistic and positive, with high self-esteem. They would agree with these statements. Do you?

	AGREE	DISAGREE
SELF-AWARENESS		
1. I'm **decisive**. I know what I want.	☐	☐
2. I'm not **impulsive**. I think before I act.	☐	☐
3. **Jealousy** is not part of my life. I am not a **jealous** person.	☐	☐
MANAGING EMOTIONS		
4. I don't feel **guilty** or **ashamed** about things I've done in the past.	☐	☐
5. **Aggressive** people don't **upset** me. I can cope with their **aggression**.	☐	☐
6. I don't get **angry** and **upset** if people disagree with me.	☐	☐
MOTIVATION		
7. I'm very **motivated**, and I set **realistic** goals for myself.	☐	☐
8. I have the **confidence**, **determination**, and **self-discipline** to achieve my goals.	☐	☐
9. My main **motivation** in life is to be **happy** and to make a difference for others.	☐	☐
EMPATHY		
10. I know when my friends feel **sad** or **depressed**.	☐	☐
11. I'm very **sympathetic** when a friend has a problem.	☐	☐
12. I think it's important to be **sensitive** to how other people are feeling.	☐	☐
SOCIAL SKILLS		
13. If friends want to do things I don't want to do, I try to be **flexible**.	☐	☐
14. I think it's good to express emotions like **grief**, **hate**, and **anger**, but in private.	☐	☐
15. **Honesty** is important to me. I'm **honest** with people unless it will upset them.	☐	☐

> *About you*

B Can you make the statements above more accurate for you by adding frequency adverbs? For example, you can say *I'm usually decisive*. Compare with a partner.

> *Word sort*

C Complete the chart with nouns and adjectives from the article. Then choose five words, and make true sentences about people you know to tell a partner.

noun	adjective	noun	adjective	noun	adjective
aggression	aggressive	guilt		realism	
	angry	happiness		sadness	
	confident	honesty			self-disciplined
depression			intelligent	sensitivity	
	determined	jealousy		shame	
flexibility			motivated	sympathy	

2 Building language

A Listen. What guesses do Paul and Ella make about why their friends are late?

Paul So where are Alexis and Sam? Do you think they might have forgotten?

Ella They couldn't have forgotten. I talked to Alexis just yesterday. They must have gotten tied up in traffic.

Paul Or, they might have had another one of their fights. Maybe Sam is off somewhere sulking, like the last time.

Ella Either way, Alexis would have called us on her cell phone.

Paul Well, she may not have remembered to take it with her. She forgets things when she's stressed out.

Ella That's true. . . . Oh, guess what? My phone's dead! So she could have tried to call and not gotten through.

Paul Oh, my gosh! The movie's about to start. We'd better go in.

> **Figure it out**

B Can you think of some possible reasons why Alexis and Sam are late? Complete the sentences below, and add one of your own. Then compare with a partner.

1. They may have _____ . 2. They might not have _____ . 3. They could have _____ .

3 Grammar *Past modals for speculation*

You can use these past modals to speculate about the past.

They **must have gotten** tied up in traffic.	= *I bet they got tied up in traffic.*
She **could have tried** to call.	= *It's possible she tried to call.*
They **may / might have had** a fight.	= *Maybe they had a fight.*

Notice the difference in meaning:

They **couldn't have forgotten**.	= *It's not possible they forgot.*
She **may / might not have remembered**.	= *It's possible she didn't remember.*

> **In conversation . . .**
>
> Affirmative statements with past modals are much more common than negative statements.

A Imagine these situations. Complete the two possible explanations for each one.

1. One of your co-workers left the company last week.
   She may _____ (find) a new job. Or she could _____ (be) fired.
2. Two of your friends broke up last month after going out together for five years.
   They may _____ (not/have) enough in common. They might _____ (have) an argument.
3. A friend didn't show up for a lunch date with you yesterday. She's normally very considerate.
   She must _____ (forget) about it. Or she could _____ (be) sick.
4. You waved to a friend in the supermarket last night. He didn't stop to say hello.
   He must _____ (not/see) me. He might _____ (be) in a real hurry.

B *Pair work* Think of two other explanations for each situation. Discuss the possibilities.

4 Vocabulary notebook *People watching*

See page 84 for a useful way to log and learn vocabulary.

1 Conversation strategy *Sharing experiences*

A Which person below has had an experience similar to A's?

A A woman on the bus today refused to move her bag so I could sit down.
B That happened to me last week.
C People can be so rude sometimes.

🎧 Now listen to Mara and Hal. What annoys them?

Mara Hey! That guy almost knocked you over getting off the elevator.

Hal Yeah. He acted like we were in his way.

Mara I get so annoyed with people like that.

Hal Me too. Like, I get upset when people push on the subway. It's so rude.

Mara Yeah, and speaking of rude people, how about the people who stand right in front of the subway doors and won't let you get off?

Hal Oh, I had that happen to me just last night. These guys were like totally blocking the doors. And when I tried to get past them, they were like, "What's your problem?"

Mara That reminds me of the time I got on the subway with my grandfather, and all these people pushed ahead of him to get seats.

Hal Isn't he like 80 years old?

Mara Yeah. I probably should have said something, but I didn't.

Notice how Mara and Hal use expressions like these to share their experiences. Find examples in the conversation.

I had that happen to me.	That reminds me (of) . . .
That happened to me.	That's like . . .
I had a similar experience.	Speaking of . . . ,

B Match the comments and responses. Then practice with a partner.

1. I complained about the service in a restaurant once, and the waiter got really angry. ____
2. At the movie last night, the people behind me were talking the whole time. It was so rude. ____
3. This woman yelled at me for cutting in line at the bank. I didn't even realize there was a line. ____
4. I used to have this friend who was late every time we met for dinner. It drove me crazy. ____

a. That's like my brother-in-law. He's never on time, and he never apologizes.
b. I had that happen to me, too. I couldn't tell if there were four lines or just one.
c. I had a similar experience with a salesperson in a department store.
d. Speaking of rude people, what about the ones who leave their cell phones on?

About you → **C Pair work** Have you had experiences like these? Take turns telling them and responding.

"I was at a restaurant today and . . ."   *"I had that happen to me. . . ."*

SELF-STUDY
AUDIO CD
CD-ROM

80

2 *Strategy plus* like

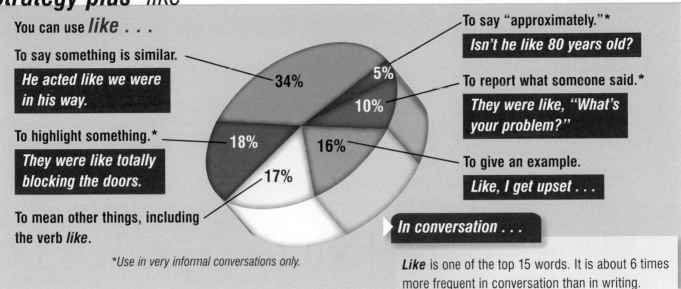

You can use **like** . . .

To say something is similar.

> *He acted like we were in his way.*

To highlight something.*

> *They were like totally blocking the doors.*

To mean other things, including the verb *like*.

To say "approximately."*

> *Isn't he like 80 years old?*

To report what someone said.*

> *They were like, "What's your problem?"*

To give an example.

> *Like, I get upset . . .*

34%   5%   10%   18%   16%   17%

*Use in very informal conversations only.

▶ **In conversation . . .**

Like is one of the top 15 words. It is about 6 times more frequent in conversation than in writing.

A Read what Amy says about a friend. Use *like* to replace the underlined words, and add other words you need. Then listen and check your answers.

"I have this friend Justin, who's very emotional. ~~For example,~~ __Like,__ one minute he's laughing, and the next minute he's – can you believe this? – _____ totally depressed. Some little thing happens, and he says, _____ , 'I'm so upset.' I guess he's – how can I say this? – _____ too sensitive. Actually, he's the same as _____ me. Maybe that's why we get along. We've been friends for about _____ 10 years."

B Listen to what else Amy says. Mark the places where she uses the word *like* with this symbol (∧). How is she using *like* in each case?

"Anyway, he gets upset easily. He gets hurt if you don't call him back right away. And then he worries that he must have said something wrong, so he calls and apologizes! And I say, 'What are you talking about?' But he's sensitive in a good way, too. When I'm upset, he's always sympathetic. He'll spend two hours listening to my problems."

3 *Listening* Similar experiences

Listen to two people talk about their experiences with taxicabs. Number the incidents in the order you hear them. Can you answer the questions?

	The cab driver hit the car in front of him. What happened next?
	The cab driver wanted to charge extra. Why?
	The cab driver was talking on the phone. What happened as a result?
	The cab driver refused to give change. How much should he have given?

4 *Free talk* Analyzing behavior

See *Free talk 8* at the back of the book for more speaking practice.

1 Reading

A When do you apologize? Think of as many situations as possible. Tell the class.

"You apologize when you hurt someone's feelings."   *"You apologize if you break something."*

B Read the article. Do you do the things the article advises?

When and How to Apologize

One key to getting along well with people is knowing when to say you're sorry. Sometimes little comments or actions can hurt or offend others. Heavy workloads and stress may keep us from seeing how our actions make others feel. The little things can add up. It doesn't take long for someone to hold a grudge and for grudges to grow into conflicts. In most cases, if someone is offended by something you do or say, it's much better to apologize right away. That solves the small problem and keeps it from getting bigger.

It's hard to apologize. Many of us are ashamed or have too much pride. Sometimes we just don't know how to do it. Here are some tips that may make it easier to say you're sorry.

Take responsibility. The first step in apologizing is to admit to yourself that you have offended someone. You may know this right away, or the other person's reaction may let you know you have done something hurtful. But you must admit you have done wrong and accept responsibility for your actions.

Explain. It's important to let the person you hurt know that you didn't mean to do harm. At the same time, you must show that you take your mistake seriously. Recognize that your actions caused a problem for the other person.

Show your regret. The other person needs to see that you have suffered, too. Come right out and say you are sorry or ashamed: "I felt bad the minute I told your secret. I'm ashamed of myself."

Repair the damage. To be complete, an apology must correct the injury. If you damaged someone's property, offer to fix it. If the damage isn't so obvious, ask, "What can I do to make it up to you?" There may be nothing concrete you can do, but the offer must be sincere: "I'll try to keep my mouth shut in the future. Meantime, let me buy you a cup of coffee." Another way to repair the damage is to send a note or a small gift.

Use good timing. Apologize right away for little things. For example, if you bump into someone, say you're sorry right away. Don't wait until the next day to apologize. However, if you have done something more serious, like insult a friend, your apology should be more thoughtful. A quick apology might seem phony. Take the time to sit down, look the person in the eye, and apologize honestly.

Remember, it's not about who "won" or who "lost." It's about keeping a strong friendship.

Source: University of Nebraska Cooperative Extension and the Nebraska Health and Human Services System

C Rewrite the sentences below. Use words or expressions from the article that have similar meanings to the underlined parts of the sentences. Then compare with a partner.

1. If you <u>stay angry with someone</u>, a small problem may turn into a bigger one.
2. Don't be <u>embarrassed about your behavior</u> if you have <u>been rude to someone</u>.
3. <u>Agree</u> that you did something wrong, and <u>understand</u> that your action was hurtful.
4. Tell the other person that you have <u>felt pain</u>, too, and then say you are sorry.
5. If the damage isn't <u>clear</u>, ask the person, "<u>How can I correct the injury I caused you?</u>"
6. If you <u>say something to upset</u> a friend, your apology should not seem <u>false</u>.

D *Pair work*   Read the article again. Discuss the questions.

1. Why is it important to apologize right away in most cases?
2. Why do some people find it hard to apologize?
3. What's a good way to apologize for a small thing? a bigger thing?
4. What new tips did you learn from the article?

2 Speaking and listening *Rude behavior*

About you → **A**   Look at the list of complaints in the survey. Which of these behaviors do you complain about most? Rank them from 1 to 8 (1 = your biggest complaint). Compare with a partner.

The Top 8 Rude Things People Do

	Me	Survey
Not clean up after pets on the street.	☐	☐
Drive with loud or missing mufflers.	☐	☐
Honk the horn unnecessarily when driving.	☐	☐
Use bad language in public.	☐	☐
Take up too many seats on the bus or train.	☐	☐
Talk on cell phones too close to others.	☐	☐
Litter the streets.	☐	☐
Drive recklessly.	☐	☐

B   Listen to Doug and Lisa talk about the survey. Number the complaints in the order in the survey. Is your order the same or different?

About you → **C**   Listen again to Doug's opinions. Do you agree? Write a response to each comment.

1. _____   3. _____

2. _____   4. _____

D *Group work*   Have you seen people do any of the things above? How did you react? Should you have acted differently? What else could you have done?

3 Writing *A note of apology*

A   Write a note of apology for something you did in the past.

Dear Mrs. Barnes,
   I just wanted to apologize for the noisy party at my apartment last weekend. I should have realized that the music was loud and that it might disturb you.
   I also wanted to say I'm sorry for not telling you about the party. I should have let you know. I promise I will be more considerate in the future.
                                        Sincerely,
                                        Jamey

> **Help note**
>
> **Writing a note of apology**
>
> I just wanted to say I'm sorry for (not) _____ing.
> I would like to apologize for . . .
> I feel I should apologize for . . .
> I promise not to . . . again.
> It was my fault entirely.

B *Group work*   Read your classmates' notes. Whose note sounds the most sincere?

People watching

Learning tip *Making connections*

When you learn new vocabulary, make a connection with something or someone you know. Think of how or when you would use the word or expression to talk about your life.

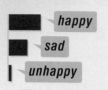
1 Think of a person you know for each of the qualities below.

1. _____ has a lot of self-confidence.
2. _____ is very good at controlling his or her anger.
3. _____ has no sympathy for people who complain a lot.
4. _____ has the motivation and determination to do well at work.

2 For each of these adjectives, write a sentence. Make a connection with someone you know or an experience you have had.

1. guilty   *My sister says she feels guilty when she eats too much chocolate.*
2. flexible   _____
3. impulsive   _____
4. sensitive   _____
5. depressed   _____
6. aggressive   _____
7. jealous   _____

3 *Word builder* Can you find the meaning of these expressions? What kind of emotion or behavior do they describe? You can use words from Unit 8 to help you.

be / feel down in the dumps _____   be set on doing something _____
be / turn green with envy _____   be heartless _____
be full of yourself _____   go nuts / bananas _____

On your own

Do some "people watching"! The next time you are on the train, in a restaurant, or out and about, watch the people around you. How are they behaving? Write notes when you get home.

He's really getting upset.

Material world

In Unit 9, you learn how to . . .

- use reported speech to say what someone has said.
- use reported questions to say what someone has asked.
- talk about possessions and money.
- report conversations you have had.
- quote other people or sources of information.

Before you begin . . .

What are your most important possessions?

Is having a lot of possessions a good thing or a bad thing?

Do you think you are materialistic?

Michael Landy, a performance artist,
preparing to granulate his TV

But Is It Art?
British artist destroys his possessions.

"**M**y goal is to destroy all my possessions. I have been making an inventory of everything I own, and it comes to 7,006 items, from televisions to reading material to records to old love letters to my Saab 900. These are the things I have accumulated in the 37 years of my life. Some of them are hard to part with, like my father's sheepskin coat, which he gave to me many years ago. But I have made a conceptual decision as an artist to shred and granulate everything."

" . . . I am also destroying artwork – my own as well as some by my friends. They said it was OK. They understand my project. At the end of this week, after my possessions are turned into granules, I want to bury them underground in a shopping center. I haven't found the right shopping center yet."

1 Getting started

A Read what British artist Michael Landy says about one of his artistic projects. What is the project? Could you do the same thing with all your possessions?

B Listen to Ginny talk about the article. Did she get the facts right?

"I read about this British artist who came up with a really unusual art project. He said his goal was to destroy all his possessions, and that he wanted to bury them in a parking lot! Can you believe it? He explained that he had been making a list of everything he owned and that it came to 17,000 items! And that he had made an artistic decision to shred and granulate everything. You can actually watch him destroying all his things. Someone explained to me that this is 'performance art.' I guess this guy really hates materialism. So do I, but I can't throw anything away. Just the same, maybe I'll stop buying so much stuff. . . . You know, I wonder why he just didn't give his stuff away."

Figure it out

C Complete these sentences to report what Michael Landy said.

1. Landy said that his goal _____ to destroy all his possessions.
2. He said he _____ to bury his possessions, but he _____ the right place yet.
3. He said some things _____ hard to part with, like his father's coat.

2 Grammar *Reported speech*

When you report the things people say, the verb tense often "shifts back."

Direct speech

Michael Landy:

"My goal **is** to destroy all my possessions."

"I **want** to bury them underground."

"My father **gave** me a sheepskin coat."

"I **haven't found** the right shopping center."

"I **have been making** an inventory."

Ginny:

"I **can't** throw anything away."

"Maybe I**'ll** stop buying so much stuff."

Reported speech

He said (that) . . .

his goal **was** to destroy all his possessions.

he **wanted** to bury them underground.

his father **had given** him a sheepskin coat.

he **hadn't found** the right shopping center.

he **had been making** an inventory.

She said (that) . . .

she **couldn't** throw anything away.

maybe she **would** stop buying so much stuff.

When you report information that is still true, the verb tense often remains the same.

Someone explained to me that this **is** what you call "performance art."

Here are some things people said about their possessions. Complete the sentences to report what they said. Compare with a partner. Do you know any people like these?

1. "I'm not at all materialistic – I have very few possessions."

    A friend of mine said that he _____ and that he _____ .

2. "My closets are all full, but I can't stop buying new clothes."

    Someone at work told me that her _____ , but she _____ .

3. "I'm always throwing things away. Once I threw out an antique vase by mistake."

    My aunt said that she _____ and that once she _____ .

4. "We're in debt because we've spent too much money on stuff for our apartment."

    My brother told his wife that they _____ because they _____ .

5. "I have a huge collection of comic books that I just don't have room for."

    One of my teachers told me that he _____ .

6. "We'll have to have a yard sale to get rid of all the junk we've been buying at yard sales."

    My neighbors said they _____ .

3 Speaking and listening *Who's materialistic?*

About you

A *Group work* Discuss the questions. How materialistic are you?

1. Do you like to have all the latest gadgets?
2. Could you live without a credit card?
3   Are you very attached to your possessions?
4. Have you ever gotten upset because you lost or broke something valuable?
5. Do you often buy things you don't need?

B Listen to Howard answer the questions above. Take notes. Then compare with a partner. How much detail can you remember?

"Howard said that he wasn't interested in gadgets at all."

1 Building vocabulary

How good are you at managing your money?

*Go through our checklist to find out. If you answer **no** to more than five questions, then you might need to do something to get things under control.*

		Yes	No
1.	Do you have a **monthly budget** and **stick to** it?	☐	☐
2.	Do you **keep track of** how much you spend each week?	☐	☐
3.	Do you give yourself an **allowance** for special "treats"?	☐	☐
4.	Do you **pay** all your **bills** on time?	☐	☐
5.	Do you **set aside money** each month in a **savings account**?	☐	☐
6.	Do you have a bank account that **pays** good **interest**?	☐	☐
7.	Do you **invest money in** reliable **stocks** and **bonds**?	☐	☐
8.	Have you **put** enough **money away** for "a rainy day"?	☐	☐
9.	Do you **pay in cash** or **by check** to avoid **charging** too much **to** a **credit card**?	☐	☐
10.	When you borrow money from friends or family, do you **pay** it **back** right away?	☐	☐
11.	If you **took out** a **loan**, would you **pay** it **off** as soon as you could?	☐	☐
12.	If you **got into debt**, would you know how to **get out of debt**?	☐	☐

A Listen and read the questionnaire from a money magazine. Answer the questions by checking *yes* or *no*. Then tally your answers. Are you good at managing your money?

Word sort

B What are your money habits? Complete the chart with sentences. Use ideas from the questionnaire, and add your own. Compare with a partner.

I do . . .	I don't . . .
I have a monthly budget.	I don't pay my bills on time.

About you

C Group work Discuss the questions in the questionnaire. Give more information about your money management techniques. Who do you think is a good money manager?

2 *Building language*

A  Listen. What did the market researcher ask John? Practice the conversation.

John I was stopped by one of those market researchers today. She was doing a survey on money.

Mother Really? What kind of things was she asking?

John She wanted to know whether I was a spender or a saver, and how I usually paid for things.

Mother Hmm. Did you tell her I pay for everything?

John Uh, no. . . . Anyway, then she asked me how many times I'd used a credit card in the past month. I told her I didn't have one, and the next thing I knew, she asked if I wanted to apply for one!

Mother But you're only 18!

John Well, I filled out the application anyway. The only thing is, . . . she asked if a parent could sign it, so . . .

Figure it out **B** How would John report these questions? Write sentences starting with *She asked me . . . .*

1. "Are you employed full-time?"   2. "How much do you spend each month?"

3 *Grammar* *Reported questions*

Direct questions	**Reported questions**
The market researcher:	She asked (me) . . . / She wanted to know . . .
"**Are** you a spender or a saver?"	**if / whether** I **was** a spender or a saver.
"How **do** you usually **pay** for things?"	**how** I usually **paid** for things.
"How many times **have** you **used** a credit card?"	**how many times** I'**d used** a credit card.
"**Can** one of your parents **sign** the application?"	**if / whether** one of my parents **could sign** it.

A Imagine the market researcher asked you these questions. Write reported questions.

1. "What is your main source of income?"   *She asked me what my main source of income was.*
2. "Are you employed full-time, or are you a student?"
3. "What is your biggest monthly expense?"
4. "How much do you spend on entertainment each month?"
5. "Have you taken anything back to a store recently?"
6. "Do you have a credit card? Are you interested in applying for one?"

About you **B** *Pair work* Take turns reporting the questions and giving your answers.

"The market researcher asked me what my main source of income was, and I told her it was my parents!"

4 *Vocabulary notebook* *Get rich!*

See page 94 for a new way to log and learn vocabulary.

1 Conversation strategy *Reporting the content of a conversation*

A This person is talking about a conversation with Bill. What do you notice about the reporting verbs?

"Bill was telling me about his new car. He was saying that it uses way too much gas."

Now listen. What do Tracy and Omar know about Kate's fiancé?

Tracy *I saw Maggie last week. She was telling me that Kate and her fiancé aren't getting along that well. They've been arguing a lot lately.*

Omar *Yeah. That's what you were saying. I've heard that he's sort of a difficult person.*

Tracy *Yeah, he is. But apparently, he bought Kate a very expensive engagement ring. An enormous diamond. Or so Maggie was saying.*

Omar *And evidently, he drives a very expensive car.*

Tracy *Right. But there's got to be something wrong, you know, if they're arguing all the time. And that's what Maggie was saying, too.*

Omar *Huh. So I wonder what'll happen.*

Tracy *Me too. . . . Maggie was at his house once, and she was saying how nice it was. But as she said, "Money isn't everything."*

Notice how Tracy talks about her conversation with Maggie. She uses past continuous reporting verbs to focus on the content rather than the actual words she heard. Also, she generally doesn't "shift" tenses. Find examples in the conversation.

"She was telling me that Kate and her fiancé aren't getting along that well."

B Report the content of the information below. Rewrite the sentences in your own way using the past continuous. Then compare with a partner.

1. A friend of yours: "I just bought a used car that I found online. You won't believe this, but it was easier than going to a dealer!"
   A friend of mine was telling me she bought a used car online. She was saying . . .

2. A classmate: "I just started this free computer class. It's really great. They teach you how to use all the latest software programs."

3. Someone from work: "Everything seemed so expensive when I went to Europe – I guess it's because of the strong euro. Everything there is just so much more expensive."

4. Your neighbor: "My daughter says she wants to marry this guy she met in college. I'm worried because they both just graduated and have student loans to pay off."

SELF-STUDY
AUDIO CD
CD-ROM

2 *Strategy plus* *Quoting information*

When you quote information you've heard, use these
expressions to identify the source:

> (As) Maggie said, " . . . "
> Maggie told me / was telling me / was saying . . .
> According to Maggie, . . .

Use these when you don't identify the source:

> Apparently, . . .   Evidently, . . .
> I was told . . .   I('ve) heard . . .
> They say . . .   I('ve) read . . .

> As Maggie said,
> "Money isn't
> everything."

> Apparently, he bought
> Kate a very expensive
> engagement ring.

Group work Ask and answer the questions. Use the expressions above in your
answers if you need to talk about what you've heard or read.

1. Who's the richest person in the world?
2. How much does the average wedding cost these days?
3. What's the best way to pay for college?
4. What's the quickest way to make a million dollars?
5. What's a good way to save money?
6. What's the most expensive thing you think you'll ever buy?

A *Isn't it Bill Gates? Apparently, he's worth billions of dollars.*
B *Yeah. I heard that he gives a lot to charities, though.*
C *Actually, my dad was telling me his boss met him one time.*

3 *Speaking naturally* *Finished and unfinished ideas*

	Finished idea:	**Unfinished idea:**
Sue was telling me about her job.	*It pays really well.*	*It pays really well . . .*

A Listen and repeat the sentences above. Notice how the intonation falls to show
the speaker has finished an idea and rises to show there's more to say.

B Listen. Which of these sentences are finished ideas (**F**)? Which sound unfinished (**U**)?
Write *F* or *U*.

1. Bob was telling me about his new job _____
2. He's been waiting tables at a restaurant _____
3. He was saying the tips were great _____
4. He's been investing all his tips in stocks _____
5. It all seems a little risky to me _____
6. I hope it pays off for him in the end _____

C Now listen to the full extract, and check your answers.

About you

D **Group work** What are some good ways to make money? How important is it to have
a well-paying job? Which jobs pay well? Which don't? Discuss your ideas.

1 Reading

A Have you ever sold any of your possessions? What did you sell? Why? Do you have any things you would like to sell? Why? Tell the class.

B Read the article. What did John Freyer decide to do with his belongings?

Everything must go online!
Iowa man inventories all his stuff to sell it off.

by A.S. Berman

Returning to Iowa City last year after a summer in New York, John Freyer came to the depressing realization that the things in the trunk of his car "were the same as what was in the trunk . . . when I (first) came to Iowa City the year before."

Determined to trim some of the clutter from his trunk and his life, Freyer launched a Web site featuring photos and detailed descriptions of his worldly possessions, each one for sale to the highest bidder.[1] "I wanted to find out what happens to me when I no longer have the things that supposedly define me," said Freyer, 28.

So, together with 50 friends, he stayed up until 4 a.m. one day last October inventorying every item in his Iowa City home. T-shirts, records, Girl Scout cookies – nothing was too mundane or too personal to escape

being slapped with a numbered inventory tag. "It was an unusual thing to see," recalls Shari Degraw, 33, a friend who attended the inventory party.

Since that night, Freyer, a part-time photographer, has been taking pictures of the nearly 1,000 items earmarked[2] for auction and posting them on an auction site. About 20 are up for bid[3] at any one time.

Visitors to his own Web site can click a button to check out what's currently on the block,[4] or to learn, for example, that someone paid $17.50 for a *Star Wars* bedspread. "When the buyer went away to college, . . . [his parents] threw out his *Star Wars* sheets, and he never forgave them," Freyer explains.

Most interesting of all, the "Browse" section of the site features

a collage[5] of Freyer's belongings. Clicking an item brings up a paragraph or two explaining how he came to acquire his kitchen table, for example. (He found it on a street corner.)

Last year, to introduce his family to his Web site, he wrapped up the Christmas gifts he bought for them and put them all up for bid separately, including links to the auctions on his site. Freyer's stepmother bought them all for about $62. "I think she's using eBay now," he says with a laugh.

Source: *USA TODAY*. March 8, 2001. Reprinted with permission.

[1] *the highest bidder* the person who offers to pay the most
[2] *earmarked* chosen
[3] *up for bid* for sale
[4] *on the block* for sale
[5] *collage* a collection of pictures

C Find the underlined words or expressions in sentences in the article. Use the context to choose the best meaning: *a* or *b*.

1. Freyer <u>launched</u> a Web site.
   a. closed
   b. started

2. What will happen when I no longer have the things that <u>define me</u>?
   a. say who I am
   b. say nothing about me

3. He began <u>inventorying</u> every item in his Iowa City home.
   a. making a list of
   b. getting rid of

4. Nothing was too <u>mundane</u> to escape an inventory tag.
   a. expensive
   b. ordinary

5. The Web site explains how he <u>came to acquire</u> his kitchen table.
   a. managed to get rid of
   b. managed to get

D Read the article again. Answer the questions.

1. What event prompted John Freyer to sell all his things online?
2. What did Freyer want to find out by selling his belongings?
3. What did Freyer and his friends do to get his things ready to sell?
4. What can visitors to Freyer's Web site find out?
5. What do you think of his project? Could you sell all your possessions online?

2 Listening and writing *I couldn't live without . . .*

A 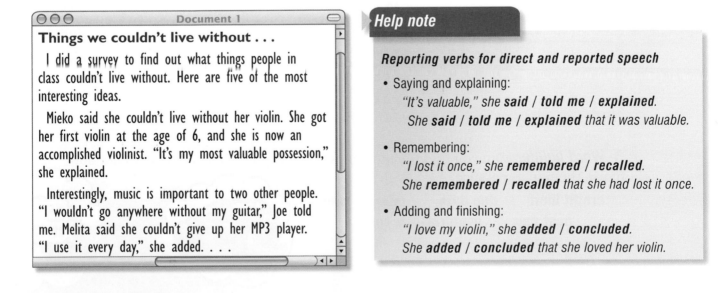 Listen to four people talk about things they couldn't live without. What do they talk about? Why couldn't they live without these things? Complete the chart.

Name	He / She couldn't live without . . .	because . . .
1. Bruno		
2. Diana		
3. Midori		
4. Max		

About you

B Listen again to these opinions. Do you agree? Write a response to each person.

1. _____   3. _____

2. _____   4. _____

C *Class activity* Ask your classmates, "What's one thing you couldn't live without? Why?" Take notes on five interesting ideas.

D Write an article from the notes you took. Use both direct speech and reported speech.

```
○ ○ ○              Document 1              ⊖

Things we couldn't live without . . .

  I did a survey to find out what things people in
class couldn't live without. Here are five of the most
interesting ideas.

  Mieko said she couldn't live without her violin. She got
her first violin at the age of 6, and she is now an
accomplished violinist. "It's my most valuable possession,"
she explained.

  Interestingly, music is important to two other people.
"I wouldn't go anywhere without my guitar," Joe told
me. Melita said she couldn't give up her MP3 player.
"I use it every day," she added. . . .
```

Help note

Reporting verbs for direct and reported speech

- Saying and explaining:
  *"It's valuable," she **said** / **told me** / **explained**.*
  *She **said** / **told me** / **explained** that it was valuable.*

- Remembering:
  *"I lost it once," she **remembered** / **recalled**.*
  *She **remembered** / **recalled** that she had lost it once.*

- Adding and finishing:
  *"I love my violin," she **added** / **concluded**.*
  *She **added** / **concluded** that she loved her violin.*

3 Free talk *Only one choice*

See *Free talk 9* for more speaking practice.

Get rich!

Learning tip *Collocations*

When you learn a new word, notice its *collocations* – the words that are used with it.
For example:

> bank account: You can <u>open</u> and <u>close</u> a bank account.
>
> allowance: You can get a <u>weekly</u> or <u>monthly</u> allowance.

In these examples, *open / close a bank account* and *weekly / monthly allowance*
are collocations.

1 Find the words and expressions that collocate with each
of the words below. Cross out the one that is *not* a collocation.

make	a credit card / a budget / a living
apply for	a job / a credit card / a bill
open	a savings account / a restaurant / a debt
pay off	a debt / a budget / a loan
invest in	checks / bonds / stocks

Talk about money

The verbs people use most
with the word **money** are:

1. spend
2. save
3. earn
4. make

2 Complete the collocations in the chart. How many ideas can you think of?

verb + noun		adjective + noun	
earn / make / spend	money	weekly / monthly	allowance
	a bank account		account
	an allowance		budget
	cash		expense
	a budget		job
	a discount		
	a bill		

3 *Word builder* Can you find the meanings of the expressions below? Find out how
to use them in a sentence.

credit limit   **due date**   **interest rate**
nest egg   **overdrawn account**

On your own

Make a wish list of some future financial
goals. What would you like to accomplish
in 5 years? in 10 years? in 20 years?

*I'd like to buy a
car in 5 years.
I'd like to buy a
house in 10 years.*

1 What would you have done?

A Complete the story using the correct forms of the verbs and expressions in the box.

apply for a credit card	get out of debt	invest money in	pay good interest	set aside money
✓get an allowance	have a budget	keep track of	pay in cash	take out a loan

When Andrew was growing up, he was careful with his money. He
got an allowance every week from his parents, and because he wanted to go
to college, he _____ every month. He opened a savings account
that _____ , so his savings grew. In college, he didn't have much
money, but he _____ and stuck to it. He _____ the
money he spent, and when he bought things, he always _____ .

But then, Andrew won $1 million in a lottery, and everything changed. He
didn't _____ stocks and bonds. Instead, he went on a spending
spree. He bought a house, a car, clothes, and computers, and he spent a lot on
travel and entertainment. Soon he had nothing left, so he _____
and started charging his everyday expenses. To pay his college tuition fees, he
_____ , which he is still paying off. Andrew has a good job now,
but he still hasn't _____ .

B Answer the questions using past modals *would have*, *should have*, *could have*,
must have, *might have*, or *may have*. Discuss your answers with a partner.

1. What should Andrew have done with the money he won?
2. Is there anything he shouldn't have done?
3. What would you have done differently? What wouldn't you have done?
4. How do you think he must have felt after he'd spent all the money?
5. Why do you think Andrew went on a spending spree?

C *Pair work* Take turns retelling Andrew's story. Use the expressions *Apparently*,
Evidently, and *I heard that*. Do any parts of it remind you of similar stories or
experiences? Share them using *That reminds me* or *That's like*.

2 How many words can you remember?

Complete the charts with nouns and adjectives. How many words can you think of
to describe personal qualities or emotions? Compare with a partner. Then ask and
answer questions using words from your charts.

Nouns		
honesty		

Adjectives		
happy		

"Is honesty important to you?"   *"Are you generally a happy person?"*

95

3 *So what were they saying?*

A Complete these quotations with a problem, and then add a solution, using the appropriate form of the verb given.

1.   John: "I went rock climbing, and I got this really big <u>hole / tear</u> in my backpack. It needs <u>to be sewn / sewing</u> (sew). Are you good at sewing?"

2.   Alice: "My kitchen faucet keeps _____ (drip), and I can't turn it off. It needs _____ (fix), but I can't afford to get a plumber _____ (do) it right now. Can you take a look at it?"

3. Robert: "I have this big oil _____ on my good jacket. I have to have it _____ (clean) before my job interview next week. Which dry cleaner's has the fastest service?"

4. Maria: "My watch has been running _____ . I've never had the battery _____ (change), so it probably needs _____ (replace). How much will a new battery cost?"

5. Hilary: "I had a car accident, and one of my doors got a big _____ in it. I've been looking for a place to get it _____ (fix). Who fixed your car after your accident?"

B Report the general content of each person's problem, using *was saying (that)* or *was telling me (that)*. Then report exactly what the person said and asked about the solution, shifting the tenses back.

John was saying that he got a hole in his backpack when he went rock climbing. He said that it needed to be sewn, and then he asked if I was good at sewing!

4 *Want some help?*

A Complete the conversations with words like *Ow, Ouch, Oops, Ooh, Ugh, Uh-oh,* and *Shoot.* Sometimes more than one answer is possible. Then practice with a partner.

1. *A* __Ow!__ I just got an electric shock. I should get that iron fixed.
   B _____ I bet that hurt. Are you OK?

2. *A* _____ My computer just crashed again. I can't understand it. It keeps happening.
   B _____ Maybe you've got a virus. Do you want me to look at it?

3. *A* _____ I'm hungry. Do you want a snack?
   B Sure. Let's see. Do you want some scrambled eggs?
   A _____ I can't stand eggs.
   B _____ I just dropped them. Oh, well, never mind.

B *Pair work* Make each sentence "shorter" if possible, and practice again. Can you continue the conversations?

A **Ow! Just got a shock. I should get that fixed.**
B **Ouch! Bet that hurt. You OK?**
A **Yeah. Think so. Guess I ought to . . .**

Self-check
How sure are you about these areas? Circle the percentages.

grammar
20% 40% 60% 80% 100%
vocabulary
20% 40% 60% 80% 100%
conversation strategies
20% 40% 60% 80% 100%

. . . .

Study plan
What do you want to review? Circle the lessons.

grammar
7A 7B 8A 8B 9A 9B
vocabulary
7A 7B 8A 8B 9A 9B
conversation strategies
7C 8C 9C

Fame

In Unit 10, you learn how to . . .

- use *if* clauses with the past perfect form of the verb to talk hypothetically about the past.
- use tag questions to check information or to see if someone agrees with you.
- talk about fame using idioms like *make headlines*.
- talk about celebrities and being famous.
- use tag questions to soften advice and give encouragement.
- answer difficult questions with expressions like *It's hard to say*.

Tiger Woods
Champion golfer

J.K. Rowling
Best-selling author

Prince William
*Second in line to the
British throne*

Shakira Mebarak
Pop singer

Midori Goto
Violinist

Before you begin . . .

What are some ways that people become famous?

What do you think is the best thing about being famous?

What is the worst thing about being famous?

The rise to fame

Unexpected Fame

Russell Watson's rise to fame was remarkable and unexpected. The English-born tenor had no formal music training, was an average student, and quit school at 16 to work in a factory. To make extra money, he sang in pubs in his spare time. Several years later, he sang in a radio talent contest and won, and his life took an amazing turn. He quit his job, got a manager, and started singing in clubs full-time. One night he ended a set of pop songs with an aria from an opera and got a standing ovation. He realized he was onto something. That's how he became a famous singer. By the age of 28, he had released his first album, *The Voice*, and had become an international star.

Dennis

It's a good thing he entered that contest. If he hadn't won, he might not have had the confidence to become a singer.

Brian

And who knows what would have happened if he had stayed in school. Maybe he would have done something entirely different.

Stephanie

Well, I think he would have found a way to be a singer. In fact, if he had continued his education, he could have had formal training and gotten an earlier start as a singer.

Anne

Yeah, maybe. Anyway, it was pretty brave of him to quit his job. If he hadn't quit and gotten a manager, he might not have had a singing career at all.

Kathleen

What amazes me is that he had enough nerve to sing something from an opera in a club! If he had only sung pop songs, he wouldn't have realized how much people loved his opera voice.

1 Getting started

A Read the newspaper article above. How did Russell Watson get his start as a professional singer?

B 💿 Listen to the students talk about Russell Watson's career. Which comments do you agree with?

Figure it out

C Can you complete the sentences? Then compare with a partner.

1. If Russell Watson had stayed in school, maybe he _____ had a very different career.
2. If he _____ won that talent contest, he might not have become a singer.

2 Grammar *Talking hypothetically about the past*

You can use sentences with *if* to talk hypothetically about the past.
Use the past perfect form in the *if* clause and a past modal in the main clause.

If + past perfect	**Past modal *would have, could have, might have,* etc.**
If Watson **had stayed** in school,	maybe he **would have done** something entirely different.
If he **hadn't won** the talent contest,	he **might not have had** the confidence to become a singer.
If he **had continued** his education,	he **could have gotten** formal music training.

Hypothetical questions about the past
What **would have happened** if he **had stayed** in school?
Would he **have become** a singer?

▶ **In conversation . . .**

People often say ***If I would have*** instead of ***If I had***, but this is not considered correct in writing.

A Read the extract about a famous author. Then complete the sentences.

Thomas J. Stanley, a university marketing professor, had written three textbooks and given seminars around the country, but he felt dissatisfied with his career. So he took time off to write *The Millionaire Next Door* with researcher William D. Danko. It hit the *New York Times* best-seller list and made them both extremely wealthy! Stanley then interviewed over 1,300 millionaires for his next best seller, *The Millionaire Mind*.

1. If Thomas Stanley __had been__ (be) satisfied with his career, he __wouldn't have taken__ (not take) time off from work, and he _____ (might not write) *The Millionaire Next Door* with William Danko.

2. If Stanley and Danko's book _____ (not be) so successful and _____ (not made) the best-seller list, Stanley _____ (might not write) his next best-selling book.

3. If Stanley _____ (continue) his job at the university, he _____ (not make) so much money. He probably _____ (not become) a millionaire himself if he _____ (not decide) to write about millionaires!

4. On the other hand, if Stanley _____ (not become) famous, he _____ (could enjoy) a quiet life as a professor.

About you **B** Write a paragraph about something lucky that has happened to you. Why was it lucky? How would your life have been different if it hadn't happened? Choose a topic below.

a hobby you started   **a job you got**   **a person you met**   **a trip you took**

Meeting my husband is the luckiest thing that has ever happened to me. We never would have met if my air conditioning hadn't broken down one Saturday. It was so hot that I decided to go to the beach, and that's where I met Jack. And Jack wouldn't have been there if . . . . If we hadn't met that day, I probably would have married my high school sweetheart.

C *Group work* Take turns reading your paragraphs and asking questions.

In the public eye

1 Building vocabulary and grammar

A 💿 Listen. How did Lana become famous? Practice the conversation.

Jon Look. Lana's at the Swan Club! You haven't seen her show yet, have you?

Kylie No, but I'd love to go. . . . She's a blues singer, isn't she?

Jon Actually, she's an **up-and-coming** rock star. She's been **in the headlines** a lot recently.

Kylie Really? I guess I'm a little out of touch, aren't I?

Jon She was on that talent show, and since then, her **career**'s really **taken off**.

Kylie Oh, I know who she is! She won the show this year, didn't she?

Jon Yeah, she did. Last year she was a student, and now she's **making headlines** as a rock singer. It's amazing, isn't it?

Kylie Huh. She must have **had connections**.

Jon I don't think so. She **got discovered** in a karaoke club by one of the show's producers. She was just **in the right place at the right time**.

Kylie I wonder what happened to the guy who won last year – Java Thomas. He's kind of **dropped out of sight**, hasn't he?

Jon Well, he **got** a lot of **bad press** when he got caught shoplifting.

Kylie Shoplifting? That wasn't too smart, was it?

Jon No, it wasn't, and his **career** has really **gone downhill**.

> **Word sort**

B Complete the chart using expressions in the conversation. Then tell a partner about someone famous. How did that person become famous?

Ways to become famous	When you're becoming famous	When things don't work out
You get _discovered_ by someone. You're just in _____ . You have _____ .	Your career _____ . You make _____ . You're _____ a lot.	Your career _____ . You get bad _____ . You _____ of sight.

> **Figure it out**

C How would Jon and Kylie make these statements into questions?

1. Lana's a singer, _____ ?
2. She won a talent show, _____ ?
3. Java Thomas got caught shoplifting, _____ ?
4. His career hasn't taken off, _____ ?

2 Speaking naturally   *Intonation of tag questions*

You're not sure and want to check something:	**You're sure and think someone will agree:**
You haven't seen her show yet, have you?	It's amazing, isn't it?

💿 Listen and repeat the questions above. Notice how the intonation rises or falls depending on the purpose of the question. Then practice the conversation in Exercise 1 again.

3 Grammar Tag questions

Tag questions are statements followed by short questions in the same tense, called "tags."

Affirmative statement + negative tag
It's amazing, **isn't it?**
She won the talent show, **didn't she?**
He's dropped out of sight, **hasn't he?**
That was a dumb thing to do, **wasn't it?**

Negative statement + affirmative tag
It's not easy to become famous, **is it?**
She didn't have connections, **did she?**
His career hasn't taken off, **has it?**
That wasn't too smart, **was it?**

Answer yes to agree.
She won the talent show, **didn't she?**
  Yes, she did.

Answer no to agree.
That wasn't too smart, **was it?**
  No, it wasn't.

A Complete the conversations with tag questions.

In conversation . . .

Negative tags are much more frequent than affirmative tags.

1. *A* You've heard of Bono, _____ ?
   B I think so. He sings with U2, _____ ?
   A Yeah. He's their lead singer. They're an incredible group, _____ ?
   B Yeah, they are. They're not American, _____ ?
   A No, they're Irish. Bono is amazing. He's done a lot to fight poverty.
   B He's raised a lot of money for charity, _____ ? I mean, he does a lot of campaigning and stuff, _____ ?
   A Oh, yeah. He's a real activist.

2. *A* When was Marilyn Monroe famous? It was in the 1950s, _____ ?
   B Yeah, but she made a movie in the 1960s, too, _____ ?
   A I think you're right. She was mainly a movie star, _____ ? I mean, she wasn't a singer, _____ ?
   B Well, she sang in some of her movies, but she was basically an actress. You've seen her movies, _____ ?
   A No, but I'd like to. It's amazing, _____ ? She died years ago, but she's still famous.

B *Pair work* How would *you* say the tags above: with rising intonation (you're checking), or with falling intonation (you think your partner will agree)? Practice the conversations.

4 Talk about it Who's hot? Who's not?

Group work Discuss the questions. Who knows the most about people in the news?

▶ Who's in the headlines these days? Why? Is anyone getting bad press?
▶ Who are the up-and-coming pop singers right now?
▶ What about movie stars? Whose careers have taken off recently?
▶ Can you think of any stars who have dropped out of sight? Why did their careers go downhill, do you think?

5 Vocabulary notebook Do your best!

See page 106 for a new way to log and learn vocabulary.

1 Conversation strategy *Giving encouraging advice*

A Look at the responses to the problem. Which advice sounds "softer" and more encouraging?

A *I can't keep up with all my homework. I'm always behind.*
B _____

    a. Well, you could talk to your teacher.   *b. Well, you could talk to your teacher, couldn't you?*

Now listen. Why is Nela thinking of dropping out of her acting class?

Steve **So, how's your acting class going?**

Nela **It's hard to say. It's fun, but I'm not learning much.**

Steve **Well, you could look for another class, couldn't you?**

Nela **Maybe. The thing is, I like the teacher, but she hardly notices me. She never gives me any feedback.**

Steve **Hmm. How can you get her attention?**

Nela **Good question. I wish I knew. Actually, I'm thinking of dropping out.**

Steve **Well, before you do that, it would be good to talk with her, wouldn't it?**

Nela **I'm not sure I want to know what she thinks! I mean, most of the other students have been acting since they were kids. Do you think that if I'd gotten an earlier start, I'd be a better actor by now?**

Steve **That's a tough one. I don't know. But you've only been in the class a few weeks. You should at least give it a chance, shouldn't you?**

Nela **You're right. I guess I should.**

Notice how Steve uses tag questions to soften his advice and give Nela encouragement. Find examples in the conversation.

"You could look for another class, couldn't you?"

B Match the problems and advice. Then role-play the conversations, and take turns giving your own advice.

1. "I have a chance to host a radio show for a week. But I'm not sure I'd be very good." ____
2. "I'd like to act in a play, but I get scared when I perform in front of people." ____
3. "I wish I could sing better. I haven't sung in ages, and my voice sounds awful." ____

a. "You could go to some auditions, couldn't you? You might get over your stage fright."
b. "Well, it would help to take some singing lessons, wouldn't it?"
c. "Well, you should give it a try, shouldn't you? It might be a lot of fun."

**SELF-STUDY
AUDIO CD
CD-ROM**

2 *Strategy plus* *It's hard to say.*

You can use expressions like these when a question is difficult to answer.

It's hard to say.
(That's a) Good question.
That's a tough one.

How can you get her attention?

Good question. I wish I knew.

Pair work Ask and answer the questions. Use the expressions above when the question is difficult to answer.

1. Do you think you'd like to be famous someday?
2. They say everybody gets 15 minutes of fame – what would you like to be famous for?
3. Would you like to perform on stage in front of a lot of people?
4. If you were a famous entertainer, would you rather be an actor, a singer, or a comedian?
5. Do you think you'd ever like to be in charge of a large company?
6. Would you like to run for a political office someday?
7. If you became famous, would you keep all of your old friends?
8. If you'd been born into a famous family, how would your life have been different?

A Do you think you'd like to be famous someday?
B That's a tough one. I'd love the attention, but . . .

3 *Listening and speaking* *Advice*

A Listen to Tom tell George about his band. Answer the questions. Choose *a* or *b*.

1. What problem is Tom's band having?
   a. They don't have enough new songs.
   b. They don't have many "gigs," or bookings.
2. Where have they played?
   a. At local clubs.
   b. In local colleges and schools.
3. What's the band's main goal right now?
   a. To get on the radio.
   b. To get discovered.

4. What idea does George suggest first?
   a. To contact a local radio station.
   b. To make a CD.
5. What does Tom think they should have done?
   a. Chosen a different name.
   b. Found a manager.
6. What does George think about their name?
   a. They should change it.
   b. It's OK as it is.

B Imagine you want to become famous. Choose an idea below, or think of your own. What would you like to achieve? What problems would you face? Make a list.

   sell your artwork   **start a band**   **start an Internet company**   **write a book**

C *Pair work* Discuss your ideas. Take turns giving advice.

A I want to write a novel, but I don't know how to get published.
B Well, you could start by going to a writing workshop, couldn't you? They tell you how to get published.

1 Reading

A Brainstorm! What personal traits do you need to become a movie star? Make a class list.

> You need to be _____.
> confident   determined   competitive

B Read the magazine article. What traits do you think Renée Zellweger has?

Renée: "I knew I'd pull through."
by Liz Smith

Fattening foods, a fake fiancé, and a broken heart – Renée has survived them all.

When you're waiting in a hotel lounge to talk to someone as red-hot as Renée Zellweger, you'd expect her entrance to cause some commotion. But the truth is, I never saw her coming.

Then again, neither did most of Hollywood. The youngest child of immigrants, Renée was the girl with the unlikely last name and cherubic face, who didn't seem destined for stardom. Her dad, a Swiss-born engineer, met her mom, a Norwegian nurse, in Denmark; the oil refinery business brought the family to tiny Katy, Texas, where Renée was raised with her older brother, Drew. When she left home to attend the University of Texas, Renée worked as a waitress until she started to land roles in little-seen movies. And when she ultimately did try her luck in Los Angeles, success did not come overnight. "I served food for quite a while," she says of her years in Hollywood restaurants.

In nearly all her films, she has struck a chord with anyone who has ever seen herself as an underdog: Not the most glamorous or the most seductive, she is simply a plucky, self-reliant survivor determined to find happiness.

Yet, just as Renée was enjoying newfound fame, she encountered controversy. Critics picked at her physique – first too plump, then too thin. Renée shrugged off the criticism, as well as the constant speculation about her love life and the false reports that she was engaged to actor Jim Carrey.

Do you feel like you've had to fight to come out on top?

RZ: In some respects. But don't we all? The thing I feel lucky about is that somehow I've always had an inner confidence. I count on me, and I've always known that I could take care of myself. I've had tough times. But there was always something there inside me that let me know I'd pull through.

Do you think a lot of that self-reliance comes from the way you were raised?

RZ: Absolutely. My family didn't have a ton of money, but we never went without when I was growing up. . . . And my father made so many sacrifices so that he could do what was best for his family.

How have fame and wealth affected you? Do you enjoy all the things you can now afford?

RZ: Here's what I really like: I like that I can make long-distance phone calls any time of day, and I can talk as long as I want and not think twice about it!

Source: *Good Housekeeping* magazine

C Find words and expressions in the article with a similar meaning to the ones below.

1. noise and activity _____
2. like an angel _____
3. find acting parts _____
4. appealed to _____
5. someone who isn't successful _____
6. brave _____
7. criticized _____
8. paid no attention to _____
9. always had what we needed _____
10. not worry about it _____

D Do you agree with these statements about Renée? Compare your answers with a partner. Say why you agree or disagree.

1. Renée had an interesting background.
2. Renée had a privileged upbringing.
3. Her success came quickly.
4. Renée is a very confident person.
5. She is greatly influenced by her father.
6. She enjoys not having to worry about money.

2 Speaking and listening *Success is . . .*

A *Pair work* How do you define success? Discuss the ideas below, and add your own.

| being famous | enjoying life every day | having an important job |
| doing fulfilling work | finding the right person to be with | having lots of money |

"I think success is being famous."   *"But not if you're famous because your parents are famous."*

B Listen to four people talk about success. What does success mean to them? Complete the sentences with ideas from above.

1. For Isabel, success is _____ .
2. For Claire, success is _____ .
3. For Carlo, success is _____ .
4. For Vivian, success is _____ .

C Listen again. Do they think they have achieved success? Complete the chart.

Names	Are they successful?	Why do they think they are or aren't successful?
1. Isabel	Yes ☐ No ☐	
2. Claire	Yes ☐ No ☐	
3. Carlo	Yes ☐ No ☐	
4. Vivian	Yes ☐ No ☐	

3 Writing *A success story*

Think of someone you know who has achieved success in some way. Make a list of reasons why he or she became successful. Then write a paragraph about him or her.

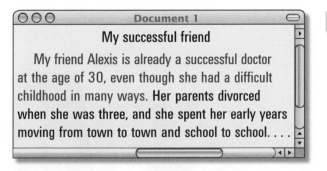

Document 1

My successful friend

My friend Alexis is already a successful doctor at the age of 30, even though she had a difficult childhood in many ways. **Her parents divorced when she was three, and she spent her early years moving from town to town and school to school. . . .**

> **Help note**
>
> **Topic and supporting sentences**
>
> **Topic sentences** state an idea or a theme.
> **Supporting sentences** add more information or give examples.

4 Free talk *Quotations*

See *Free talk 10* for more speaking practice.

Vocabulary notebook

Do your best!

The words most likely to be used with **fame** are:

1. fame **and fortune**
2. **gained** fame
3. **hall of** fame
4. **claim to** fame
5. **achieved** fame

Learning tip *Learning idioms*

Idioms are expressions in which the meaning isn't obvious from the individual words. When you learn a new idiom, it helps to write an example sentence that explains or clarifies its meaning.

1 Match these sentences containing idioms with the explanations on the right.

1. He's been <u>in the headlines</u> a lot lately. <u>c</u>
2. He's getting a lot of <u>bad press</u>. ___
3. He's an <u>up-and-coming</u> actor. ___
4. His <u>career</u> has really <u>taken off</u>. ___
5. He <u>got discovered</u> very young. ___
6. He <u>had connections</u> in the industry. ___
7. He's really <u>dropped out of sight</u>. ___
8. His acting <u>career</u> is <u>going downhill</u>. ___

a. His career is going really well.
b. People think he's going to be a great actor.
c. He's been in the news.
d. You don't hear about him anymore.
e. He knew people who helped his career.
f. He's getting fewer and fewer acting roles.
g. He started his career at a young age.
h. The news media are criticizing him.

2 Word builder Now write explanation sentences for these idioms. Find out the meaning of any expressions you don't know.

1. A lot of young people really <u>look up to</u> pop stars.

_____

2. My friend is a great singer. She's going to <u>go a long way</u>.

_____

3. Some rock bands are still <u>going strong</u> after 20 or 30 years.

_____

4. That young actor is going to <u>make a name for himself</u>.

_____

5. She <u>knew the right people</u>, so she got the part.

_____

6. He came to the city to try to <u>get into show business</u>.

_____

On your own

Make a list of 10 famous people you like. Can you use a different idiomatic expression about each person?

I really look up to him.

1. Yao Ming

106

Trends

In Unit 11, you learn how to . . .

- use the passive of the present continuous and present perfect.
- link ideas to express a contrast, reason, purpose, or alternative.
- talk about trends in society, the environment, and the workplace.
- refer back to points made earlier in a conversation.
- use more formal vague expressions like *and so forth* and *etc*.

Before you begin . . .

Do any of these issues affect your city or country? Is the situation changing? What is the trend?

- traffic congestion
- working parents
- pollution
- aging population
- urban development
- unemployment

What social changes have you noticed recently?

1

"A lot of people are obsessed with losing weight and eating healthy foods. So the fast-food chains have been forced to change their menus. Now you can get salads and healthy stuff there, as well as burgers and fries."

– **James, Miami**

2

"Well, one thing is the shortage here of people with skills in technology. There's a big demand for that now, so skilled workers are being recruited overseas, and then they're being brought in to fill the jobs."

– **Tomoko, Osaka**

3

"I think, like everywhere else, the main thing is the spread of technology. I mean, almost everyone has a cell phone and an MP3 player, . . . and wireless Internet access is being made available all over."

– **Chen, Taipei**

4

"Well, people are talking about losing their jobs. In many places, unemployment is going up, and a lot of people have been laid off. And that's partly because their jobs are being outsourced to workers in other countries."

– **Fiona, London**

5

"We have a lot of problems with traffic congestion. Fortunately, a lot of new highways have been built, and there's a new monorail, but the problem hasn't been completely solved. So, commuting can still be a real problem."

– **Somchai, Bangkok**

6

"Well, more and more young people are being encouraged to go to college, which is good. It can be tough, though, because tuition fees have just been increased, and we're not being given enough financial support."

– **Estela, Monterrey**

1 Getting started

A Listen. What trends or changes have these people noticed in their society recently?

Figure it out

B Rewrite the sentences, starting with the words given. Then compare with a partner.

1. People are forcing fast-food chains to change their menus.   Fast-food chains . . .
2. They've made Internet access available all over.   Internet access . . .
3. Companies are laying off a lot of people.   A lot of people . . .
4. They haven't given us enough financial support.   We . . .

2 Grammar *Passive of present continuous and present perfect*

Use the active form of a verb to focus on the "doer" or cause of the action.	**Use the passive form to focus on the "receiver" of the action.**
Companies **are recruiting** workers overseas.	Workers **are being recruited** overseas.
They **are making** Internet access available.	Internet access **is being made** available.
Companies **have laid off** a lot of people.	A lot of people **have been laid off**.
They **haven't solved** the traffic problem.	The traffic problem **hasn't been solved**.

A Rewrite the sentences, using the passive forms of the underlined verbs. Then compare with a partner.

1. They're selling a lot more organic foods in supermarkets now. Public demand <u>is forcing</u> supermarkets to stock healthy foods, like low-salt and low-fat products.

   A lot more organic foods are being sold in supermarkets now. . . .

2. They <u>have</u> totally <u>rebuilt</u> parts of the city. They've <u>put up</u> lots of new offices and hotels in the last five years, and they've <u>knocked down</u> a lot of older buildings. They <u>haven't solved</u> the parking problems, though.

3. They're <u>advertising</u> new tracking gadgets for cars. They're <u>selling</u> them to parents who want to keep track of their kids when they borrow the car. They've <u>developed</u> them with GPS (Global Positioning System) technology.

B *Group work* Which of the trends above and on page 108 are happening where you live? Which trends do you think are good? Which are not? Explain.

"A lot of our city has been rebuilt. I think it's good because a lot of jobs have been created."

3 Speaking naturally *Reducing auxiliary verbs*

The education system **is** being reformed.	(system's being)
The education system **has** been reformed.	(system's been)
A lot of new schools **are** being built.	(schools're being)
A lot of new schools **have** been built.	(schools've been)

A Listen and repeat the sentences above. Notice the reduction of the auxiliary verbs.

B Listen and complete the sentences. Are they true in your country? Are they good ideas? Discuss your views with a partner.

1. More schoolteachers _____ employed.
2. More women _____ encouraged to study science and engineering.
3. English _____ made a required course in all high schools.
4. Workers at some companies _____ told to learn a second language.
5. Older people _____ encouraged to go to college.
6. Education _____ given top priority by the government.

1 Building vocabulary and grammar

A Complete the article with words and expressions from the box. What do you learn?

| air pollution | drought | environment-friendly | landfill | toxic chemicals |
| biodegradable | energy-saving | global warming | natural resources | water consumption |

What can YOU do to protect the environment?

Although environmental problems can seem overwhelming, there is hope if everyone gets involved in protecting our _____ . Here's what you can do:

Consume less energy. Climates are changing and ocean levels are rising because of _____ . This growing problem is due to increased levels of carbon dioxide in the atmosphere as a result of the burning of oil, coal, and gas. In order to save electricity, use _____ lightbulbs, and turn the air-conditioning down or off when possible. To conserve gas or oil, turn down the heat by 2°F (1°C). You'll also cut 10% off your bill!

Don't use your car if you don't have to, because cars consume energy and also cause _____ . So instead of driving everywhere, use public transportation. Or ride a bicycle – you'll get good exercise and help improve your city's air quality.

Avoid toxic cleaning products. Look for _____ brands, even if they're more expensive. This helps cut down on the _____ that contaminate our rivers and oceans, and that are generally harmful to the environment.

Recycle all of your garbage. Recycle newspapers, magazines, batteries, and all packaging such as cartons, bottles, cans, and plastics so that they don't end up in a _____ . Packaging that is not _____ can take years to decompose. And recycling paper, glass, plastic, and metal saves energy.

Conserve water. Even though 1.2 billion people in the world lack safe drinking water, people in developed countries use 15 bathtubfuls of water a day! You can cut your _____ in half by taking showers instead of baths. And water your lawn only once a week. Some people water lawns daily in spite of water shortages and _____ warnings.

Word sort ▸ **B** What environmental problems are you concerned about? What are you doing to help? Complete the chart with ideas from the article, and add your own. Compare with a partner.

I'm concerned about . . .	*I'm . . .*
global warming.	using energy-saving lightbulbs.

Figure it out ▸ **C** Can you choose the correct expression to complete each sentence? Compare with a partner. Are the sentences true for you?

1. I turn down the air-conditioning **in order to / so that** use less electricity.
2. I buy rechargeable batteries **in spite of / even though** the extra cost.
3. **Because / Because of** cars cause air pollution, I always take public transportation.

2 Grammar Linking ideas

Contrast:	**Although / Even though** environmental problems are overwhelming, there is hope.
	Some people water their lawns daily **in spite of / despite** drought warnings.
Reason:	Climates are changing **because of / as a result of / due to** global warming.
	Carbon dioxide levels are increasing **because** we are burning oil, coal, and gas.
Purpose:	Turn down the air-conditioning **(in order) to** save electricity.
	Recycle garbage **so (that)** it doesn't end up in a landfill.
Alternative:	Use public transportation **instead of** driving your car.
	Take showers **instead of** baths.

Notice:

in order to / to + verb

although / even though / because / so that / so + clause

in spite of / despite / because of / as a result of / due to / instead of + noun (or verb + -ing)

A Link the ideas in these sentences using expressions from the grammar chart. How many ways can you complete each sentence? Compare with a partner.

1. _In order to / To_ save water, you should take showers _instead of_ baths.
2. _____ building new highways for cars and trucks, the government should spend money on public transportation.
3. Global warming isn't being taken seriously enough, _____ rising ocean levels and floods.
4. When homes near the ocean have been destroyed _____ a flood, the owners shouldn't be allowed to rebuild in the same place.
5. More money should be invested in wind, solar, and wave power _____ we don't need to burn so much coal, gas, and oil.
6. Private cars should be banned from cities _____ people are developing serious health problems _____ air pollution from automobiles.
7. _____ it would cost me more to drive my car, I would be happy if they raised gasoline taxes _____ cut down on gas consumption

About you → **B** **Pair work** Discuss the opinions above. Which ones do you agree with?

3 Talk about it Saving the planet

Group work What are the most serious environmental problems today? Rank these problems from 1 to 6 (1 = most serious). What is being done to solve them? What else could be done?

_____ air and water pollution _____ depletion of oil reserves _____ garbage in landfills
_____ global warming _____ nuclear waste disposal _____ endangered species

4 Vocabulary notebook Try to explain it!

See page 116 for a useful way to log and learn vocabulary.

Like I said, . . .

1 Conversation strategy *Referring back in the conversation*

A Choose the best expression to complete what Paula says below.

Ted It seems that families these days don't have enough money unless both parents work. But then child care becomes a major cost.

Don Things are changing, though. Parents are being offered more benefits, like flexible schedules.

Paula But like you said, Ted, benefits / schedules / child care can be a big problem.

Now listen to what else Don, Ted, and Paula say. What is changing for working parents?

Don As I was saying, things are changing. There are more benefits for working parents, like paternity leave, unpaid family leave, and so forth.

Paula That's true. Like, in the last five years or so, more people have been encouraged to work from home – telecommuting and so on. That helps, too.

Don Going back to what you said about child care, Ted, day-care centers are now being provided free by some companies.

Paula So parents can just bring their kids to work.

Ted But very few companies offer this benefit.

Paula That's a good point. Don, you mentioned unpaid leave earlier. I think it's great that parents can take time off without losing their jobs.

Ted I agree. But unpaid leave means less money. And like I said, families need two incomes.

Don Just the same, I think the trend is for companies to offer more benefits, incentives, etc., to attract and keep good employees.

Notice how Don, Ted, and Paula use expressions like these to refer back to things said earlier. Find examples.

| As / Like | I said / I was saying . . . |
| Going back to what | you said / you were saying . . . |

You / I mentioned . . . earlier.

B Listen to more of their conversation. Write the expressions they use.

Paula Yes, and _____ , Don, companies now offer paternity leave, not just maternity leave. I mean, it's only fair. Then a father can stay home with a new baby, too.

Ted I think companies could do more. But _____ , Paula, about telecommuting, if more people could work from home, maybe child care wouldn't be such a problem.

Don Yeah. And _____ , Ted, unpaid family leave means less money for a family, so maybe telecommuting is a better alternative for parents.

2 Strategy plus *and so forth*

In more formal settings, use vague expressions like **and so forth, and so on,** and **etc.** instead of informal expressions like *and things like that.*

etc. = et cetera

The trend is for companies to offer more benefits, incentives, etc.

> **In conversation . . .**

Informal vague expressions like **and things like that** are more common than formal ones.

	and things like that
	and so forth
	and so on
	etc.

About you → Add an appropriate expression to each opinion below. Then discuss with a partner. Do you agree?

1. Almost everyone can work from home these days with the Internet, e-mail, _____ .
2. These days, people don't want to work long hours, like in the evenings, on weekends, _____ .
3. Companies need to reward employees better, with bonuses, raises, _____ .
4. Another good incentive is time off, like more vacation time, personal days, _____ .
5. A lot of people are being forced to work harder, with longer hours, less time off, _____ .
6. Work is getting more stressful. People now have to learn new skills, do new jobs, _____ .

A I agree that people can work from home these days with the Internet, e-mail, and so on.

B That's true for some jobs, but not all jobs can be done at home, like construction work, acting, etc.

3 Speaking and listening *Changes we see*

About you →

A *Pair work* Look at the list of trends in the workplace. Which ones do you think are good ideas? Which are not? Discuss with a partner.

- paternity leave
- unpaid leave
- day-care centers
- flexible hours
- monitoring e-mails
- working from home

B Listen to four conversations about trends. What topics do the people talk about? Write them in the chart.

What is the trend?	**Is it a good one?**	**Why or why not?**
1. _____	☐ Yes ☐ No	_____
2. _____	☐ Yes ☐ No	_____
3. _____	☐ Yes ☐ No	_____
4. _____	☐ Yes ☐ No	_____

C Listen again. Do the people think the trends are good? Why or why not? Check (✓) the boxes and write the reasons in the chart.

4 Free talk *Save the world!*

See *Free talk 11* for more speaking practice.

1 Reading

A Which of these gadgets and new technologies do you use regularly? Add other examples. Tell the class.

- blogs
- podcasts
- MP3 player (digital music player)
- DVR (digital video recorder)
- PDA (personal digital assistant)
- satellite radio

B Read the article. What gadgets and new technologies do Natalia and Andreas use?

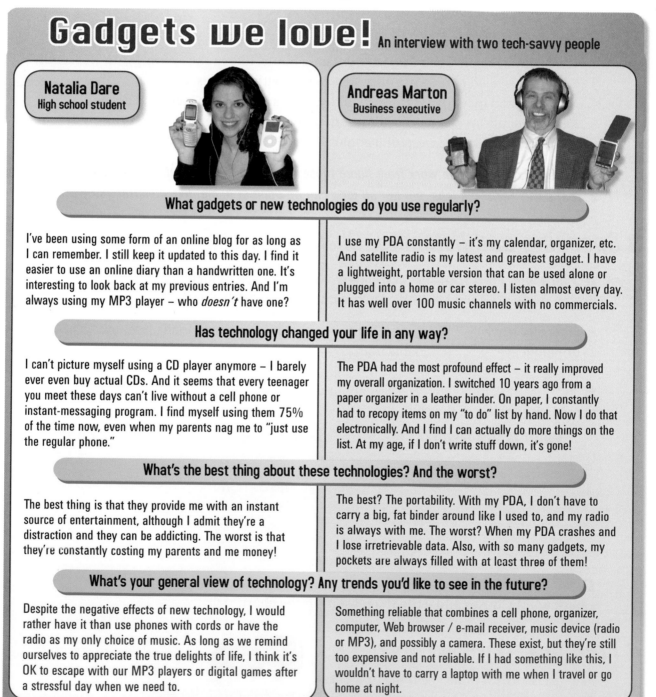

Gadgets we love! An interview with two tech-savvy people

Natalia Dare
High school student

Andreas Marton
Business executive

What gadgets or new technologies do you use regularly?

I've been using some form of an online blog for as long as I can remember. I still keep it updated to this day. I find it easier to use an online diary than a handwritten one. It's interesting to look back at my previous entries. And I'm always using my MP3 player – who *doesn't* have one?

I use my PDA constantly – it's my calendar, organizer, etc. And satellite radio is my latest and greatest gadget. I have a lightweight, portable version that can be used alone or plugged into a home or car stereo. I listen almost every day. It has well over 100 music channels with no commercials.

Has technology changed your life in any way?

I can't picture myself using a CD player anymore – I barely ever even buy actual CDs. And it seems that every teenager you meet these days can't live without a cell phone or instant-messaging program. I find myself using them 75% of the time now, even when my parents nag me to "just use the regular phone."

The PDA had the most profound effect – it really improved my overall organization. I switched 10 years ago from a paper organizer in a leather binder. On paper, I constantly had to recopy items on my "to do" list by hand. Now I do that electronically. And I find I can actually do more things on the list. At my age, if I don't write stuff down, it's gone!

What's the best thing about these technologies? And the worst?

The best thing is that they provide me with an instant source of entertainment, although I admit they're a distraction and they can be addicting. The worst is that they're constantly costing my parents and me money!

The best? The portability. With my PDA, I don't have to carry a big, fat binder around like I used to, and my radio is always with me. The worst? When my PDA crashes and I lose irretrievable data. Also, with so many gadgets, my pockets are always filled with at least three of them!

What's your general view of technology? Any trends you'd like to see in the future?

Despite the negative effects of new technology, I would rather have it than use phones with cords or have the radio as my only choice of music. As long as we remind ourselves to appreciate the true delights of life, I think it's OK to escape with our MP3 players or digital games after a stressful day when we need to.

Something reliable that combines a cell phone, organizer, computer, Web browser / e-mail receiver, music device (radio or MP3), and possibly a camera. These exist, but they're still too expensive and not reliable. If I had something like this, I wouldn't have to carry a laptop with me when I travel or go home at night.

C Read the article again, and find the things below. Then compare with a partner.

1. two reasons Natalia likes her online blog
2. two ways she communicates with people
3. a gadget she never uses
4. three disadvantages of her use of technology
5. three things Andreas likes about his satellite radio
6. the gadget that changed his life the most
7. two things he doesn't like about his current gadgets
8. what his next purchase might be

About you ➔ **D** *Group work* Discuss the questions in the article.

Can you agree on:
- the gadget or new technology that is most useful in your daily lives?
- the biggest change technology has made in your lives?
- the most important advantage of gadgets and new technology?
- the biggest disadvantage of new technology?
- a new gadget or technology that would make your lives better in the future?

2 *Listening and writing* *Changing your life*

A 💿 Listen to three people talk about technology, and number the pictures. Why do they like the technology? Write one reason under each picture.

B Think of a new technology that you use. Why do you like it? How has it changed your life? Is there any disadvantage to using it? Write a short article about it.

○○○   **Document 1**

How my PDA has changed my life

    More and more people are using PDAs to organize their lives, and I am part of this trend. My PDA is my office, computer, address book, cell phone, music center, and camera – all in one. I need fewer gadgets than I did before.

    Thanks to my PDA, things that I used to do at home or at work can now be done on the move. It lets me contact people and access the Internet from anywhere.

    However, one disadvantage is that I feel like I'm always "at work," and . . .

> **Help note**
>
> **Describing trends**
>
> **More and more** *people are using PDAs.*
> *I need* **fewer** *gadgets than I did before.*
> *Desktop computers have become* **less** *popular.*
> *The number of PDAs is* **increasing / growing**.
> *Sales of computers are* **decreasing / declining**.
> *PDAs are* **increasingly** *being used for Internet access.*

C *Class activity* Read your classmates' articles. Which changes are the most interesting?

Try to explain it!

Learning tip *Writing definitions in your own words*

When you learn a new word or expression, you can write a definition or explanation in your own words to help you remember its meaning.

1 Look at these expressions from the article on page 110. Match them with their definitions or explanations.

1. The **atmosphere** refers to ___e___
2. **Carbon dioxide** is a gas in the atmosphere ____
3. If you **consume** something, ____
4. **Air quality** refers to ____
5. When there is a **water shortage**, ____
6. If something is **toxic** to the environment, ____
7. When you **recycle** something, ____
8. If something **decomposes**, ____

a. you use it up, and it can't be used again.
b. there isn't enough water for people.
c. you use it again instead of throwing it away.
d. it contaminates or pollutes the environment.
e. the air around the Earth.
f. that is produced when things burn or decay.
g. it decays, or breaks down into simple elements.
h. how much pollution is in the air.

2 Complete the sentences to define or explain these expressions from page 110.

1. A **landfill** is a place where _____ .
2. **Global warming** means that the temperature of the Earth _____ .
3. **Toxic chemicals** are substances that _____ .
4. If a product is **environment-friendly**, that means it doesn't _____ .
5. If something is **biodegradable**, it will _____ .
6. **Water consumption** refers to how much _____ .
7. A **drought** is a period of time when _____ .
8. **Air pollution** means that _____ .

3 *Word builder* Find out the meaning of these words and expressions. Then write a sentence to define or explain each one.

> deforestation   fossil fuels   pesticides
> extinction   hybrid cars   renewable energy
> the greenhouse effect   the ozone layer

On your own

Help save the environment, and learn new words at the same time! Write notes to yourself in English reminding you to turn off the lights, recycle bottles, and so on. Post the notes around your home.

Careers

In Unit 12, you learn how to . . .

- introduce information with *What* clauses and long noun phrases as subjects.
- use the future continuous and future perfect to talk about the future.
- talk about planning a career and different jobs people do.
- introduce what you say with expressions like *The best part was . . . .*
- say *I don't know if . . .* to introduce ideas and involve other people in your conversation.

Before you begin . . .

Which of these areas of work are hard to get into? Which are easier?

Which are the highest paid? Which are the most popular with your friends?

- the media
- hotel and tourism
- medicine
- law
- finance
- entertainment
- social work
- teaching
- trades (carpentry, plumbing)

Finding a career

What's the best way to go about choosing a career?

Laura

I think the first thing to do is to decide on an area you're interested in. And then do some research to find out what jobs you can do in that area. I mean, what I'd do first is talk to people and find out what jobs they do. And maybe find out more on the Internet. The main thing you need is lots of information.

Jacob

Yeah, for sure. What you should do is think about what you really enjoy doing with your time. And then see if you can make a career out of it. The good thing about that is you end up with a job you love. I guess what I'm saying is that you need to choose a career you'll really like.

Jason

Right. And one thing I would do is see a career counselor and take one of those personality tests to find out what your strengths and weaknesses are. And then the career counselors . . . well, what they do is tell you what kinds of jobs you'd be good at.

Jenny

Another thing you can do is apply for an internship with a company. The advantage of that is that you get some work experience while you're still in school. What a friend of mine did was interesting. What she did was call up a bunch of companies and offer to work for free on her vacations. She got some great experience that way.

1 Getting started

A Listen. What ideas do these students suggest for choosing a career? Which are the best ideas?

Figure it out → **B** How did the students actually make these points?

1. *Laura* First, you need to decide on an area you're interested in.
2. *Jacob* I guess I'm saying you need to choose a career you'll really like.
3. *Jason* I would see a career counselor.
4. *Jenny* A friend of mine did something interesting. She called up a bunch of companies.

2 Grammar   What clauses and long noun phrases as subjects

What clauses and long noun phrases introduce important information. They are often the subject of the verb *be*, which can be followed by a word or a phrase (noun, adjective, or verb), or by a clause.

What clauses

What you need is lots of information.
What my friend did was interesting.
What I would do is talk to people.
What I'm saying is (that) you need to choose a career you'll really like.

Long noun phrases

The main thing you need is information.
Something my friend did was interesting.
The best thing to do is (to) talk to people.
The good thing about that is (that) you end up with a job you love.

A Once you've chosen a career, how do you go about getting your dream job? Choose the best expression on the right to complete each sentence.

1. I think ___the first thing to do___ is to get some work experience. _____ is contact a company I was interested in. You know, _____ was good. She started out in the mail room at a newspaper and ended up as a reporter.

> what I would do
> ✓ the first thing to do
>   what my friend did

2. You know, _____ is go to a job fair. _____ is to meet the recruiters. They sometimes interview you right there, and _____ is you might get hired immediately.

> the main reason to do that
> one thing you can do
> the good thing about that

3. Well, _____ is a good résumé. _____ is get mine done professionally. _____ is that you can make a really good first impression.

> what you really need
> the advantage of that
> what I'd do

4. You know, _____ is ask all my friends and family if they had any personal contacts. _____ is that they might be able to help you get an interview. _____ is good contacts.

> the main thing you need
> the good thing about that
> what I'd do first

About you → **B** *Group work* How would you go about getting your dream job? Discuss ideas.

A **What I'd do first is ask my friends and family for personal contacts.**
B **That's a good idea. It helps to have connections.**
C **Yeah, and then what you need is a really good résumé to send out.**

3 Speaking naturally   Stressing I and you

Anne *What would you do if you found your dream job and then hated it?*
Matt *I don't know. What would **you** do if **you** hated your dream job, Cate?*
Cate *I have no idea what I'd do.*
Enzo *I know what **I** would do. I'd quit immediately. Life's too short. How about **you**?*

Group work Listen and repeat the conversation. Notice how *I* and *you* are sometimes stressed to make clear who you are talking about. Continue the discussion in your group.

1 Building vocabulary and grammar

A Listen and read the interviews. What career plans do these students have?

Where do you think you'll be working five years from now?

Well, I'll have finished my degree in media studies by then, and what I really want to do is get a job in **communications**. You won't be seeing me on TV or anything – I'm not cut out for that – but I may be working in, like, **publishing** or **journalism** as an **editor** or writer or something. Or maybe I'll have gotten a job in **advertising** or **public relations**. That would be fun. **– Ashley**

Well, in two years, I'll be graduating with a degree in **nursing** – so I'll be working in the field of **health care**. I'd like to be a **psychiatric nurse**, but I'm not sure. Hopefully my wife will have graduated from medical school by then, too. She'd like to be a **pediatrician** . . . or else a **surgeon**. **– Albert**

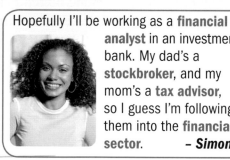

Hopefully I'll be working as a **financial analyst** in an investment bank. My dad's a **stockbroker**, and my mom's a **tax advisor**, so I guess I'm following them into the **financial sector**. **– Simone**

I won't be doing what I'm doing now – **telemarketing** – that's for sure! This fall, I'll be starting a degree in **business management**, so in five years, I'll have graduated and gotten a job in the **construction industry**. I probably won't have had much experience, but I'll be working with **civil engineers**, **contractors**, **construction workers**, and so on. **– Jesse**

I don't really know. I just hope I'll be using my languages. I might be working as an **interpreter** or a **translator** – or maybe I'll be working in the **travel industry**. **– Cheryl**

B Make word webs for these areas of work. Add more jobs. Which jobs do you think would be interesting? fun? well paid? rewarding? Compare with a partner.

Construction industry   Financial services   Media and communications   Medicine and health care

civil engineer

C Can you make these sentences true by changing the underlined words? Compare with a partner.

1. Five years from now, Ashley will <u>be studying for</u> her degree in media studies.
2. At this time next year, Albert <u>will</u> have graduated with a degree in nursing.
3. Cheryl <u>will</u> have gotten a job as a translator five years from now.
4. Jesse <u>will</u> be working in telemarketing in five years.

2 Grammar *The future continuous and future perfect*

Use the future continuous for ongoing activities in the future.
> I'll **be working** in health care.
> I **won't be working** in this job.

Also use it for events you expect to happen.
> I'll **be graduating** in two years.
> I'll **be starting** a degree this fall.

You can use *might* and *may* instead of *will*.
> I **may be working** in publishing.

Use the future perfect for events that are in the past when you "view" them from the future.
> My wife **will have graduated** by then.
> I probably **won't have had** much experience.

▶ **In conversation . . .**

The future continuous is much more common than the future perfect.

A Complete the conversations using the future continuous or future perfect. Then practice with a partner.

1. *A* What do you think you'll _____ (do) five years from now?
   B I might _____ (work) as an accountant. I'll probably _____ (pass) all the exams by then. How about you?
   A By then I'll _____ (graduate) – I hope to graduate in two years. So I probably will _____ (start) my PhD, but I won't _____ (finish) it by then.

2. *A* What do you think your life will be like in ten years?
   B I hope I'll _____ (find) a partner by then and we'll _____ (buy) our own home. I also hope we'll _____ (start) a family and I'll _____ (take) care of the kids, but I may _____ (work) part-time, too.

3. *A* What do you think you'll _____ (do) when you're 60?
   B Well, I hope I won't _____ (work). I suppose I'll _____ (retire) by then, so I hope I'll _____ (enjoy) life.
   A Me too. Maybe by then I'll _____ (buy) a yacht, and I'll _____ (sail) every day!

About you → **B Pair work** Ask and answer the questions. Give your own answers. Do you have similar hopes and dreams?

3 Talk about it *Working lives*

Group work Discuss the statements. Do you agree with them?

Ten years from now, . . .
▶ more people will be working from home.
▶ people will be working fewer hours, and they'll have more leisure time.
▶ people will be retiring at a younger age.
▶ people will still be learning English to help them with their careers.
▶ it will be more difficult for graduates to find work.

4 Vocabulary notebook *From accountant to zoologist*

See page 126 for a new way to log and learn vocabulary.

The best part was . . .

1 Conversation strategy *Introducing what you say*

A Can you complete the conversation with your own ideas?

    A   *I have a part-time job working in a fast-food place. The best part is* _____ .
    B   *Yeah? What I heard was* _____ .

Now listen to Hiro and Jenn. What was Jenn's summer job? How did she like it?

Hiro	**Didn't you work in that theme park last summer?**
Jenn	**Yeah. In the ticket booth for the concert arena.**
Hiro	**Really? How was it? The reason I ask is I was wondering about applying for a job there myself.**
Jenn	**It was good. I mean, the best part was that I got to go on all the rides for free. I don't know if you know, but you get a free season pass.**
Hiro	**Cool.**
Jenn	**Yeah. And what I thought was really good was I got to see a lot of the concerts and meet some of the performers backstage.**
Hiro	**Great. Now, what I heard was that it's hard to get a job there.**
Jenn	**Well, yeah. What I was going to tell you was that they have a job fair in the spring. I don't know if you're familiar with one, but you go around the park and interview for different jobs.**
Hiro	**Yeah? Maybe I should go to that.**

Notice how Hiro and Jenn introduce what they say with expressions like these. Find the expressions they use.

What I thought was good was (that) . . .	*The best part is / was (that) . . .*
What I heard / read was (that) . . .	*The reason I ask is (that) . . .*
What I was going to tell you / say was (that) . . .	

B Complete the conversation using the expressions above. More than one answer is possible. Then listen and notice what Hiro and Jenn actually say.

Jenn   Yeah. It's a good way to get hired.
Hiro   But _____ they like to hire people who have worked there before. You know, people with experience.
Jenn   Yeah. But you've worked in restaurants and things, right? _____ I know they're always looking for servers.
Hiro   They are? That would be good.
Jenn   It's hard work, but _____ you get good tips.
Hiro   Well, I'm going to apply for sure. Hey, by the way, _____ I got accepted to grad school next year!

SELF-STUDY
AUDIO CD
CD-ROM

2 Strategy plus *I don't know if . . .*

I don't know if . . .
can introduce a statement,
often to involve the other
person in the topic.

*I don't know if you know, but
you get a free season pass.*

> **In conversation . . .**

Some of the most common expressions
with **I don't know if** are:

I don't know if you've (ever) heard . . .
I don't know if you're familiar with . . .
I don't know if you've (ever) seen . . .

A Match the two parts of the sentences below.

1. I don't know if you've ever sent out your résumé, ____
2. I don't know if you've read *Volunteer Vacations*, ____
3. I don't know if you've heard about Tom, ____
4. I don't know if you've worked in a restaurant, ____
5. I don't know if you're familiar with jobs.com, ____
6. I don't know if you've ever thought about starting your own business, ____

a. but it's really hard work.
b. but he just got hired as an interpreter.
c. but companies often don't bother to reply.
d. but you can post your résumé on the site.
e. but you can get a start-up loan at the bank.
f. but it has all kinds of ideas for opportunities to work overseas.

About you → **B** *Pair work* Take turns telling each other something interesting about jobs, using the ideas above. Start with *I don't know if . . . .* Can you continue each conversation?

3 Listening and speaking *What's she doing now?*

A Listen to Marina give an interview about her job, and choose the correct answers. Do you think Marina is happy in her job? Why or why not? Tell the class.

1. Where do you think Marina works?
   a. In an art gallery.
   b. In a furniture store.
   c. In an advertising company.

2. What does she spend most of her time doing?
   a. Talking to customers.
   b. Writing leaflets.
   c. Designing Web pages.

3. What subject did she study in college?
   a. Software development.
   b. Advertising.
   c. Journalism.

4. How does she feel about working in advertising?
   a. It's a good area to work in.
   b. She doesn't want to start at the bottom again.
   c. It's too competitive.

About you → **B** *Group work* Discuss the questions.

■ What do you think would be an ideal job? Why?
■ Are there any jobs that you really wouldn't want to do? Why not?
■ Have you had any interesting or unusual work experience?
■ Have you applied for any jobs recently? Is it difficult to get into that line of work?
■ Would you like to have your own business? What kind of business would you have?

"You know what I think would be an ideal job? To be one of those people who cast actors for roles in movies. The best thing is that you'd get to meet all the stars."

1 Reading

A Brainstorm! What would you do to prepare for a job interview? Make a class list.

> I'd make sure I had a nice outfit to wear.
> One thing I'd do is find out as much as I could about the company.

B Look at the four interview questions in the article. How would you answer them? Compare ideas with a partner. Then read the article. How would you change your answers?

Perfect answers to tough and tricky interview questions
by Julia Savacool

You've got one chance to make a first impression. Here, you'll learn how to answer the questions a recent survey of 2,000 managers found to be most common.

"Describe your ideal job."
"This is your chance to show you know the business," says Nancy Behrman, president of Behrman Communications in New York City. "Your answer should convey excitement for the specifics of what my company does." In other words, talk job content, not ideal office hours.

"Why do you want to leave your current position?"
Be honest but positive. "Speaking in a frustrated tone about your current boss makes me nervous," says Behrman. "I'd rather hear your enthusiasm about taking your career to the next level."

> **Why do you want to leave your current position?**
> a. I need more money.
> b. The hours are terrible.
> c. I need a new challenge.
> d. My boss is a slave driver.
>
> **Your final answer should be c.**

"Tell me about yourself."
"Don't start with the year you were born," jokes Alison Corazzini, head of recruiting at J.P. Morgan in New York City. "It's a waste of time to walk the interviewer through your whole résumé. What she wants to know is what about you makes sense for her firm. Highlight a few experiences that might not stand out on paper."

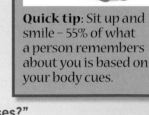

Quick tip: Sit up and smile – 55% of what a person remembers about you is based on your body cues.

"What would you say are your strengths and weaknesses?"
Strengths are easy – you know what you're good at, and don't be afraid to talk about it. As for flaws, "Don't share your worst trait, but saying your biggest weakness is that you pay too much attention to detail – I don't buy it," says Corazzini. Go ahead, admit you've had a problem with taking on too much, but explain how you've learned to balance your workload. Ultimately, managers would rather hire someone who knows her weak spots than someone who thinks she has none.

Source: Originally published in *Glamour* Magazine

C Answer the questions. Then compare answers with a partner.

1. When interviewers say "Describe your ideal job," what are they really asking?
2. Based on the advice, what is the best way to answer questions about your previous job?
3. Why is body language important?
4. What do recruiters want to know about you? What's the best way to tell them?
5. What does the article suggest you do after revealing a weakness?

2 *Listening and writing* *A fabulous opportunity!*

A  Read the job advertisement. Can you guess the missing words? Then listen to Maria talk about the ad with her friend Alex. Were any of your guesses correct?

WANTED: **Local Tour Guides for Australian Travel Company**

Are you looking for a _____ summer job? Do you enjoy meeting people from other _____ ? Are you interested in your local _____ ? Are you _____ ? Can you speak good _____ ? Do you like to _____ ? If you answered *yes* to these questions, write to Jane

Cowley, _____ of **18⁺ TRAVEL**, and tell her why you would be an _____ guide. Send letter and recent _____ to P.O. Box 25 at the *Daily Times*. Successful applicants will receive excellent _____ and a generous benefits package.

B Listen again. Answer the questions.

1. What does Maria think is the best thing about the job?
2. Why does Alex think Maria would be good at the job?
3. What does Maria have to do to apply?
4. What does Alex think Maria should do first?

C Imagine you want to apply for the job above. Write a letter of application to the company.

Dear Ms. Cowley,

Re: Local Tour Guide position

I am applying for the position of Local Tour Guide, which was advertised in the *Daily Times* on April 1. My strongest qualification for this position is that I speak fluent English.

As you can see from the enclosed résumé, I have had previous experience in this type of work with students from abroad who attend university summer programs. It was my responsibility to help them with any problems they had. In addition, I have . . .

I am enthusiastic about pursuing a career in the tourist industry. I believe that I would be an excellent guide and that tour groups would enjoy my sense of humor and positive attitude.

I would welcome the opportunity to meet with you. I can be reached at 917-555-1954 every day from 12 until 5. Thank you for your time and consideration.

Sincerely,

Jun Lee Jong

Jun Lee Jong
Enclosure

> **Help note**

Writing an application letter

- Use the name of the person if you can.
- Write a subject line to show what the letter is about.
- Opening paragraph: State what the position is, how you heard about it, and what your strongest qualification for it is.
- Middle paragraph(s): Say why you are suitable – give more information about your qualifications or experience, and describe your strengths.
- Closing paragraph: Restate your interest and offer to meet for an interview. Thank the person for his or her time.
- End the letter like this.

D *Group work* Read your classmates' letters. Who do you think should get the job as a tour guide?

3 *Free talk* *Job fair*

See *Free talk 12* for more speaking practice.

Vocabulary notebook

From accountant to zoologist

Learning tip *Word building with roots and collocations*

When you learn a new word, you can expand your vocabulary quickly by learning

- other words with the same root.

journalism   journalist

- some common collocations.

political journalist
broadcast journalist
freelance journalist

1 Complete the chart with the areas of work and the jobs.

Area of work	Job
accounting	accountant
architecture	
	carpenter
counseling	
	dentist
design	
editing	
	engineer
financial analysis	
	interpreter
law	
	manager
	nurse

Area of work	Job
pediatrics	
	photographer
physiotherapy	
	plumber
psychiatry	
	psychologist
	publisher
sales	
stockbroking	
	surgeon
telemarketing	
	translator
	zoologist

2 Word builder Match the words in **A** with the words in **B** to make common collocations. How many jobs can you make? Can you add any more words to make different job combinations?

A

civil	psychiatric
construction	social
laboratory	systems
pediatric	

B

analyst	technician
engineer	worker
nurse	

On your own

Find a newspaper that lists employment opportunities or job advertisements. Write the names of 20 different jobs in English.

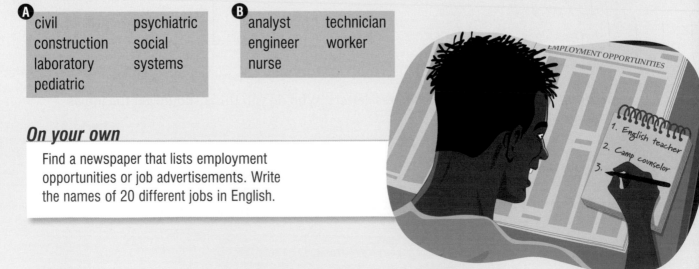

Touchstone checkpoint
Units 10–12

1 Talking about jobs

Match the two parts of each sentence. Then discuss them with a partner. Add ideas and expressions like *and so on*, *and so forth*, and *etc.*

1. Being a surgeon is very rewarding, __c__
2. Stockbrokers are under a lot of stress _____
3. It's easy to get health-care jobs these days _____
4. Workers are being brought into the country _____
5. Plan your career in five-year blocks _____
6. More students are taking media studies, _____
7. There are fewer telemarketing jobs _____

a. even though there are few jobs in this field.
b. in order to fill all the jobs in construction.
c. in spite of the long hours you have to work.
d. so that you can set realistic goals.
e. because of the shortage of nurses.
f. as a result of outsourcing to other countries.
g. due to all the competition in the field.

"I imagine being a surgeon is rewarding, in spite of the long hours and the stress and so on."

2 How many words can you think of?

A Add six words and expressions to each category, and compare with a partner.

Being famous	
in the headlines	

The environment	

B *Pair work* Choose four items from each category to use in a conversation. How many different expressions can you remember to introduce what you say?

A *I don't know if you've heard, but Angelina Jolie is in the headlines right now.*
B *Oh, yeah. What I heard was she recently . . .*

3 What will life be like in 2030?

A Complete the sentences using the future continuous or future perfect.

1. Hopefully, by 2030, people __will be buying__ (buy) environment-friendly products, and we _____ (use) energy-saving gadgets, so we _____ (live) in a cleaner environment.
2. Ideally, we _____ (stop) global warming by then. We _____ (not use) fuels like coal anymore. We _____ (discover) newer, cleaner, and more efficient fuels.
3. By 2030, people _____ (eat) healthier food, and the number of obese people _____ (decrease).
4. Because we _____ (live) longer, the percentage of older people in society _____ (rise) by then.

B *Group work* Discuss the sentences. Refer back to what people say, with expressions like *As you said*, *Like you were saying*, and *Going back to . . . .* Add your opinions.

4 What if . . . ?

"I applied for an internship at a public relations company after college. At the end of my interview, they offered me a job. Now, twenty years later, I'm still there, and I'm vice president."   **– Alice**

"I was bored with my job at the bank, so I saw a career counselor and took some personality tests. They showed I was creative! So I went into advertising, and I love it."   **– Martin**

"I was going to major in math at college, but I got sick the first week and had to drop out. In the hospital, I got interested in nursing, and so now, here I am – a pediatric nurse."   **– Alfonso**

A Read the comments above. How might these people's lives have been different? Write sentences using *if* + the past perfect form and *would have, could have,* or *may / might have.*

If Alice hadn't applied for an internship at that company, she wouldn't have ended up working there.

B *Pair work* Tell about three big decisions you've made in life. Ask and answer hypothetical questions. If a question is difficult to answer, use an expression like *Good question.*

5 Check it out.

What do you know about your partner? Complete the sentences, adding tag questions. Then ask your partner.

1. You live in _____ , __*don't you*__ ?
2. You've studied English for _____ years, _____ ?
3. You don't like _____ music, _____ ?
4. You're a _____ , _____ ?
5. You went to _____ on vacation once, _____ ?

6 Any suggestions?

Complete the sentences using the passive of the present continuous or present perfect. Then role-play with a partner. Take turns making suggestions.

1. "We *'re being given* (give) too much homework these days."
2. "I _____ (ask) to do volunteer work, but I'm too busy."
3. "I _____ (promote) at work, but I prefer my old job!"
4. "People _____ (lay off) at work recently. I'm worried because I _____ (pay) more than my co-workers."

A We're being given too much homework these days.
B You could talk to your teacher about it, couldn't you?

1 Choose a classmate to interview for an article in a magazine, and think of interesting things to ask him or her. Complete the questions below.

Questions for: _____   **Answers** _____

1. How long have you been _____ ? _____
2. When did you last _____ ? _____
3. Have you ever considered _____ ? _____
4. What's your favorite _____ ? _____
5. Have you ever tried _____ ? _____
6. Where do you hope you'll _____ ? _____
7. What do you like to _____ ? _____
8. What's the nicest _____ ? _____
9. Who do you _____ ? _____
10. What do you remember about _____ ? _____
11. What were you doing _____ ? _____
12. How did you end up _____ ? _____

2 **Pair work** Now ask your interview questions. Take notes on your partner's answers.

3 **Class activity** Share the most interesting questions and answers with the class.

Group work Discuss the questions. Do you agree on your answers?

1. Which cars are popular right now? What kind of car would you like to own? Why?
2. What clothing styles are in fashion right now? Do you like the new styles as much as last year's styles?
3. Which hairstyles are trendy now? How have they changed over the last couple of years? Has your own hairstyle changed?
4. What bands are popular right now? Are there any bands that you don't hear about as much as you used to?
5. Are there any diets or kinds of food that are popular? Is your diet as healthy as it could be?
6. What kinds of exercise are popular?
7. How have your personal tastes changed over the last five years – for example, in fashion, music, and food?
8. What do you like now that you didn't like two years ago?

A **Well, those big SUVs are popular right now. It seems like you see them everywhere.**

B **Right. I'm not sure I'd like to own one, though. They're not as economical as a car.**

C **That's true. But don't you think it would be fun to drive one?**

1 Pair work Plan a presentation on local customs for visitors to your country, or another country that you both know about. Use the topics below to give you ideas, and add more of your own.

Greeting people

Eating traditional food

Visiting someone's home

Shopping

2 Class activity Now take turns making your presentations. As you listen to each one, write down one piece of information that you think visitors will find particularly useful. Be sure to ask questions at the end if you didn't hear or understand something properly.

"Welcome to Brazil. If you are visiting our country, there are some useful things you need to know about our local customs. Brazilian people are very friendly, and they always greet you with a warm smile. . . ."

Class activity You are going to play a message game. Follow the instructions below step-by-step.

Step 1 Write your name on a piece of paper, fold it, and put it on your teacher's desk. Then pick another piece of paper from the pile. Read the name on the paper, but keep it a secret.

Step 2 Think of a place you would like to go with the person whose name you picked. Complete the chart with information about your plans.

a place you would like to go	
what day	
what the event is supposed to be like	
a time and place to meet	
what to wear	
how much it costs	
one thing to bring along	
what the weather is supposed to be like	

Step 3 Ask another classmate to pass on the message to the person whose name you picked. Explain the details of your invitation.

"Could you pass on a message to Pablo? Tell him I'd like to go to the movies with him tonight. There's a new action movie playing at the Roxy, and it's supposed to be really good. Tell him to meet me at 6:00 at . . ."

Step 4 Another classmate will tell you a message to pass on to someone else. Listen carefully and try to remember all the details.

Step 5 Pass on the message that you were told. Did you remember everything?

Step 6 Someone else will pass on a message to you. Listen carefully for all the details. Then consider the invitation. Do you want to accept? Are you free? Tell the class.

"Carla asked me to go to a concert tomorrow night. It's a jazz group, and they're supposed to be really good. We're supposed to meet at 7:00 at the concert hall. Jeans are OK, and tickets cost $10. I should bring an umbrella because it's supposed to rain. But unfortunately, I can't go. I'm supposed to be going out with my sister tomorrow night. . . ."

Step 7 When the person you invited out tells the class about your invitation, check the information in your chart. How well did your messenger pass on your message?

Free talk 5　Lawmakers

1 Pair work Imagine you are on a committee that proposes new laws to the government. Choose one of the topic areas below. Think of reasons for and against each of these possible new laws.

Marriage vows　People shouldn't be allowed . . .
- to get married until they have taken a marriage-preparation course.
- to get a divorce until they have been married for 10 years.
- to marry before the age of 21.

Education　A law should be passed . . .
- that prohibits students from quitting school before the age of 18.
- to make everyone learn at least two foreign languages.
- to ban examinations for students under 16.

Driving　A law should be passed . . .
- to prevent people over 70 from driving a vehicle.
- to ban high fees for car insurance for young people.
- to stop companies from making cars that go faster than the speed limit.

2 Group work Find another pair who chose the same topic as you. Compare your arguments for and against the laws. Which laws do you agree to propose to the government? Which do you decide to drop?

Free talk 6　Can you believe it?

Pair work Take turns telling each other about these unusual beliefs and strange events.

Can you think of . . .

1. something you used to believe as a child but you don't believe now?
2. something you are superstitious about?
3. something that happened to you that was really good luck?
4. a time when you dreamed about something and then it came true?
5. a time when you were able to tell what someone else was thinking?
6. a time when you experienced a strange coincidence?

A *I used to believe in the tooth fairy. Every time I lost a tooth, I'd put it under my pillow. In the morning, the tooth would be gone, and there would be money there instead. I really believed it was from the tooth fairy.*

B *I did too. I didn't realize it was my parents who gave me the money until I was about ten. And I was so disappointed!*

D　Free talk 5 and Free talk 6

Free talk 7 — What's the solution?

Group work Look at each of the problems below, and discuss the questions.

- What needs to be done?
- What advice would you give to someone in this situation?
- Have you ever experienced a problem like this?
- What would you do in this situation?

A *The carpet needs to be cleaned immediately. It looks like someone spilled grape juice on it.*

B *Yeah. They should probably get it cleaned professionally.*

C *Something like that happened to me once. I spilled tomato juice on the couch. I tried to clean it, but there's still a stain on it.*

Free talk 9 — Only one choice

1 Pair work Imagine you can have *one* item from each of these sets. Tell your partner which item you'd choose and why.

1. *For summer . . .*
   a. a surfboard
   b. a gas barbecue
   c. a season pass to a theme park

2. *For your lifestyle . . .*
   a. a brand-new sports car
   b. a studio apartment
   c. $20,000 in cash

3. *For a once-in-a-lifetime opportunity . . .*
   a. a trip to Antarctica
   b. a chance to meet the celebrity of your choice
   c. a personal makeover

4. *For entertainment . . .*
   a. a shelf full of books
   b. an MP3 player
   c. a large-screen TV

5. *For fun . . .*
   a. a digital video camera
   b. a telescope
   c. a mountain bike

6. *For a challenge . . .*
   a. scuba-diving lessons
   b. a chance to run a marathon
   c. an opportunity to start your own business

2 Group work Join another pair. Tell them what your partner chose and why. Then listen to the other pair's choices. Did you choose any of the same items?

"For summer, Maddie said she wanted a season pass to a theme park so that she could go every week. Actually, she asked if she could have four passes so that her friends could go, too!"

Group work Read the situations below. Then discuss them and answer the questions.

- Why did the people act this way, do you think?
- How do you think they must have felt?
- Do you think they reacted appropriately?
- What do you think they should have done?
- What else could they have done?
- Would you have acted differently?

Sarah's situation Sarah found out that her boyfriend, Allan – who she had been dating for four years – had no intention of marrying her. She really thought they would get married someday. They had a huge argument, and as she was getting out of his car, she scratched the door with her keys. He called the police.

A *Well, I think Sarah must have been really upset if she scratched Allan's car.*
B *And he must have been really angry about it because he called the police.*
C *Well, I don't think Sarah should have done that. She could have just broken up with him and left.*

Joe's situation Joe moved into a new apartment a few months ago. His new neighbors played loud music late at night, and Joe had to get up early every morning for work. Joe asked his neighbors to turn the volume down, but they didn't. Finally, Joe decided to teach his neighbors a lesson, and he started to play loud music early every morning when they were trying to sleep. They no longer speak to each other.

Margie's situation Margie was in a movie theater when her cell phone rang. She answered the call and talked loudly for about five minutes. The people sitting next to her asked her to be quiet, but when she continued to talk, they called the theater manager. He asked her to leave the theater. She refused and started shouting at him. Then someone in the row behind threw a box of popcorn at her.

1 Group work Look at the quotations below. Which ones do you agree with?
Which one is your favorite? Why?

> A man is a success if he gets up in the morning and gets to bed at night, and in between does what he wants to do.
> — Bob Dylan

> Success is a state of mind. If you want success, start thinking of yourself as a success.
> — Dr. Joyce Brothers

> Success is to be measured not so much by the position that one has reached in life as by the obstacles which he has overcome.
> — Booker T. Washington

> I realized early on that success was tied to not giving up. . . . If you simply didn't give up, you would outlast the people who came in on the bus with you.
> — Harrison Ford

> **Always aim for achievement, and forget about success.**
> — **Helen Hayes**

> I am busy living in the "right now" and trying to do my best every day. That to me is success.
> — Yoko Ono

2 Can you think up your own definition of "success"? Complete the sentence below.
Success is _____ .

3 Class activity Now go around the class, and find out your classmates' definitions.
Choose the two you like best, and write them down with your classmates' names.
Then share your new "quotations" with the class.

1 Group work How would you like to help save the world? Make plans to create an organization that could fight for an important cause. Answer the questions below.

1. What is your organization called? Choose a name.
2. What is the purpose of your organization? What cause are you fighting for?
3. What are you going to ask people to do to support your cause?
4. What will you do with any money you raise?

2 Class activity Present your cause to the class. Each person in the group can take part in the presentation, or you can choose a spokesperson. Answer questions from your classmates about your organization.

Save the butterfly!
We want to open a live butterfly sanctuary. . . .

Water for the world!
We need to provide water to areas of the world where there are droughts. . . .

DON'T STEP ON THE GAS!
Walk, bike, or take the bus – but don't drive! . . .

PICK IT UP!
When you see garbage on the ground or by the road, don't leave it there. . . .

ENERGY AWARENESS
There are many ways to stop wasting energy in our daily lives. . . .

1 Look at the different job ads below. Choose a job that you'd like to apply for, and prepare for a job interview. Think of answers to the following questions.

- Why are you interested in this job?
- What experience and qualifications do you have that would help you in this job?
- What qualities do you think someone needs in order to do this job well?
- What would you say are your main strengths and weaknesses?
- How would you like to see your career progress over the next five years?

HELP WANTED

❶ OFFICE ASSISTANT

Office assistant needed in busy head office of an international trading company. Must have good computer skills, be well organized, and be able to work independently on a wide variety of tasks. No office experience necessary. Positive attitude a must.

❷ TUTORS

Tutors needed in various subjects to teach first-year college students who need extra help. Math, English, sciences, and music. Also computer studies and art. Only patient and reliable people should apply. Flexible hours and excellent pay. College degree required.

❸ STUDENT COUNSELORS

Student counselors needed by local foreign student exchange agency to assist students from overseas with all aspects of life in a foreign country. Will need to help communicate with host families and with schools. Ability to speak one or more foreign languages and excellent people skills required. Experience living abroad would be a plus.

❹ TECHNOLOGY STAFF

Major technology company needs part-time staff for exhibitions around the country. Duties include setting up displays and explaining products to the public. An interest in computers and technology is a must. If you enjoy travel, meeting people, and working hard, please apply.

2 *Group work* Act as an interview "panel," and interview each person for the job they want to apply for. Take turns asking the questions above. At the end of the interview, hold a group vote, and decide if the person should be hired.

A ***So, Alicia, what job are you applying for?***

B ***I'm applying for the job at the technology company.***

C ***OK, so why are you interested in this job, Alicia?***

B ***Well, mainly because I'm very interested in computers and technology in general. One thing I would really like to do is explain all the different products to people. . . .***

Self-study listening

Unit 1

A *Track 1* Listen to the conversation on page 6. Juan and Bryan are telling Kim a story.

B *Track 2* Listen to the rest of their conversation. Check (✓) true or false for each sentence.

	True	False
1. Juan and Bryan saw a bear.	☐	☐
2. Kim's story is about a time she was camping.	☐	☐
3. Kim was eating dinner when she heard the noise.	☐	☐
4. Kim didn't have any food in the tent.	☐	☐
5. Kim decided that if she saw a bear, she would run.	☐	☐
6. A bear was looking for something to eat.	☐	☐

Unit 2

A *Track 3* Listen to the conversation on page 16. Tracy and Omar are shopping for a birthday gift.

B *Track 4* Listen to the rest of their conversation. Circle the correct words.

1. **Tracy / Tracy's sister** subscribes to music magazines.
2. Tracy's sister **has / doesn't have** broad tastes in music.
3. Tracy's sister and Omar's brother like **the same / different** kinds of music.
4. Omar thinks his brother and Tracy's sister **would / wouldn't** like each other.
5. Tracy **is / isn't** invited to the party.

Unit 3

A *Track 5* Listen to the conversation on page 26. Hilda and David are talking in the classroom.

B *Track 6* Listen to the rest of their conversation. Choose the right answer. Circle **a** or **b**.

1. What does David think Hilda should do?
   a. Travel in the U.S.
   b. Study in the U.S.
2. How long would Hilda like to be away?
   a. For the summer.
   b. For a year.
3. When does Hilda need to apply by?
   a. The end of the month.
   b. The beginning of the summer.
4. Who should Hilda talk to?
   a. Another teacher.
   b. Another student.
5. What does she have to send in with her application?
   a. A teacher recommendation and an essay.
   b. A teacher recommendation and some money.

Unit 4

A *Track 7* Listen to the conversation on page 38. Grant and Martin are talking about surprise parties.

B *Track 8* Listen to the rest of their conversation. Check (✓) true or false for each sentence.

	True	False
1. Grant was supposed to organize a surprise party for Martin.	☐	☐
2. Martin was planning to work late on his birthday.	☐	☐
3. Grant has already booked a band for the party.	☐	☐
4. Martin likes the band that's supposed to play at his party.	☐	☐
5. Martin wants Grant to cancel the party.	☐	☐

Unit 5

A *Track 9* Listen to the conversation on page 48. Jin Ho and Celia are talking about security cameras.

B *Track 10* Listen to the rest of their conversation. Circle the correct words.

1. Jin Ho says a lot of people **don't know about** / **don't like** the cameras.
2. Celia thinks speeders should be **punished** / **given a second chance**.
3. The fine for speeding is **$60** / **$600**.
4. Jin Ho **has already paid** / **is going to pay** the fine.
5. Jin Ho agrees that speed cameras **work** / **don't work** as a deterrent.
6. Jin Ho needs Celia to **lend him some money** / **give him a ride**.

Unit 6

A *Track 11* Listen to the conversation on page 58. Carlos is asking Nicole about her bad dreams.

B *Track 12* Listen to the rest of their conversation. Complete the sentences. Circle *a* or *b*.

1. Carlos says your sleep is affected by . . .
   a. the direction your bed faces.
   b. the room you sleep in.
2. Nicole can't move her bed because . . .
   a. it's too heavy.
   b. it won't fit anywhere else.
3. Some people believe bad dreams . . .
   a. come in through windows.
   b. come in through doors.
4. Dream catchers are . . .
   a. people who have bad dreams.
   b. window decorations.
5. Carlos saw dream catchers . . .
   a. in a friend's room.
   b. in stores.
6. Nicole is planning to . . .
   a. buy a dream catcher.
   b. make a dream catcher.

Unit 7

A *Track 13* Listen to the conversation on page 70. Kayla is helping Hector hang a picture in his apartment.

B *Track 14* Listen to the rest of their conversation. Check (✓) true or false for each sentence.

	True	False
1. Hector and Kayla have both shopped at the thrift store.	☐	☐
2. Hector had to get the picture frame fixed.	☐	☐
3. Hector will work on the bookcase himself.	☐	☐
4. Hector knew the clock needed fixing when he bought it.	☐	☐
5. Kayla thinks the clock's battery needs replacing.	☐	☐
6. Hector and Kayla fix the clock.	☐	☐

Unit 8

A *Track 15* Listen to the conversation on page 80. Mara and Hal are talking about manners.

B *Track 16* Listen to the rest of their conversation. Circle the correct words.

1. They think it's rude when young people sit at the **front** / **back** of the bus.
2. Mara felt sorry for the woman because she looked **tired** / **sad**.
3. Mara offered the woman her seat **because it was special** / **to be polite**.
4. The woman **sat in the seat** / **gave it away**.
5. Mara **was glad** / **regretted** that she had offered the woman her seat.

Unit 9

A *Track 17* Listen to the conversation on page 90. Tracy and Omar are talking about friends.

B *Track 18* Listen to the rest of their conversation. Complete the sentences. Circle *a* or *b*.

1. Omar wants enough money . . .
   a. for a nice car.
   b. for entertainment.
2. Kate doesn't like it when her fiancé . . .
   a. spends money.   b. makes money.
3. Kate's fiancé wants to live in . . .
   a. a big apartment.   b. a big house.

4. Omar says most couples fight . . .
   a. about money.   b. about family.
5. Maggie and her boyfriend have . . .
   a. gotten married.   b. broken up.
6. Maggie and her boyfriend fought . . .
   a. about money.
   b. about family and friends.

Unit 10

A *Track 19* Listen to the conversation on page 102. Steve is asking Nela about her acting class.

B *Track 20* Listen to the rest of their conversation. Check (✓) true or false for each sentence.

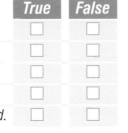

	True	False
1. Steve didn't complete a writing class in college.		
2. Nela's friend got her job through connections.		
3. Steve enjoys his job.		
4. Steve would like to hire an assistant.		
5. Nela thinks Steve could possibly be hired by her friend.		

Unit 11

A *Track 21* Listen to the conversation on page 112. Don, Paula, and Ted are discussing changes in the workplace.

B *Track 22* Listen to the rest of their conversation. Circle the correct words.

1. Ted thinks telecommuting is good for **parents** / **young people**.
2. Paula's company allows **telecommuting** / **flexible hours**.
3. Ted also talks about **job sharing** / **sick leave** for parents.
4. Paula **is** / **isn't** interested in a telecommuting job.
5. Don thinks flexibility in the workplace is a **good** / **bad** thing.

Unit 12

A *Track 23* Listen to the conversation on page 122. Hiro and Jenn are talking about summer jobs.

B *Track 24* Listen to the rest of their conversation. Choose the right answer. Circle *a* or *b*.

1. How long will Hiro be in school?
   a. One more year.
   b. Two more years.
2. What program is Hiro going into?
   a. Arts management.
   b. Marketing.
3. What has Jenn been studying?
   a. Business.
   b. Marketing.

4. What will Hiro be studying this fall?
   a. Business law.
   b. International communications.
5. What should Jenn tell the university?
   a. About her job goals.
   b. About her job experience.
6. What will Jenn be doing this summer?
   a. Working as a salesperson.
   b. Working as a manager.

Unit 1

Kim That's so funny! What did you think the noise was?

Bryan I don't know. We didn't bother to find out! Maybe a bear?

Juan I just remember running because Bryan started running.

Kim I almost saw a bear once. Sort of.

Bryan What do you mean?

Kim I was camping with my family. And one night, my sister and I were in our tent, just going to sleep, and suddenly we hear this noise outside. There was something walking around the campsite, knocking things over.

Juan Oh, no!

Kim So my sister goes, "It's a bear. It's looking for food," and then she says, "I'm glad we don't have any food in here."

Bryan Yeah. Bears can rip right through a tent if they smell food.

Kim I know! But then I had to tell my sister that I actually had some candy bars with me. So now we're both terrified. And we decide to look outside the tent and run if we see a bear!

Juan So? What was it?

Kim Something looking for food, all right, but it was my dad!

Unit 2

Tracy A magazine subscription's a really nice gift.

Omar Yeah. I wonder which one to get, though.

Tracy You know, my sister gets music magazines – *Music Monthly, Music News, Pop World*. I could ask her which one's the best.

Omar OK. That'd be great. Now, what kind of music is she into?

Tracy Oh, all kinds of stuff. Hip-hop, soft rock, soul, classical, . . .

Omar Pretty much everything, then. Sounds like she likes music as much as my brother does.

Tracy Yeah. And the same kinds of music, too.

Omar You know, maybe we should get them together sometime. Don't you think they'd get along?

Tracy Oh, yeah. Definitely. They've got a lot in common.

Omar Maybe I should invite her to my brother's birthday party.

Tracy Great idea. She'd love it. She's pretty outgoing, you know.

Omar OK. I'll send her an invitation.

Tracy Um . . . what about me? Aren't you inviting me, too?

Omar You? Yes, I'm inviting you! You chose his gift, after all!

Unit 3

Hilda It sounds like you really love it here.

David I do. You know, you should think about spending a year at school in the U.S. I think you'd enjoy living there.

Hilda Oh, I don't know. To tell you the truth, I think it would be hard to be away from my family for so long.

David Of course. Well, maybe you'd like to go for a shorter time. Many universities offer summer programs, you know.

Hilda Going away just for the summer sounds better. I'd like that.

David In fact, there's still time to apply for this summer. You just need to mail your application by the end of the month.

Hilda This summer? Really? Well, I don't have any plans yet. . . .

David Do you know Patricia in my Monday class? She's going to study in New York this summer. You should talk to her.

Hilda I will. What else do I have to send in with the application?

David An essay and a recommendation from your English teacher.

Hilda OK. Well, would you be able to check my essay . . . and maybe write a recommendation for me, too?

David Of course I would! I'd be happy to help.

Unit 4

Grant So, you really don't like surprise parties, huh?

Martin No, I don't. Why? Wait a minute – are you planning one?

Grant Well, I was supposed to. We were going to do something for you after work, but if you really don't like the idea, . . .

Martin I'd rather not. I was just going to get off work a bit early and have a quiet evening with a couple of friends. Have you already made all the arrangements and everything?

Grant Well, just a few, like we booked the place and invited people, and Brad was going to book a band. But I don't know if he got around to doing that, so . . .

Martin Huh. Which band?

Grant It's a local band – The Beat. They're supposed to be good.

Martin You're kidding! The Beat? They're excellent. I really like them. Well, you guys probably can't get out of that. . . .

Grant I don't know. We might be able to . . .

Martin Well, wait. I think I like the sound of this surprise party.

Grant Yeah? So, do I get the feeling we should go ahead with it?

Martin Oh, sure. I'm looking forward to it now. The Beat . . . cool!

Unit 5

Jin Ho Another thing is, a lot of people don't know the cameras are there – like speed cameras on the highway.

Celia Yeah, but I don't have a problem with speed cameras. For two reasons – number one, speeding is dangerous. That's just a fact. And, two, it's against the law. If people get caught speeding, they should be punished.

Jin Ho Well, yeah, that's true. But the point is, people ought to be told where the cameras are. And secondly, they should be told it's a $600 fine if they get caught.

Celia Well, you've got a point there. Wow. $600 is expensive! I had no idea. So how do you know how much the fine is?

Jin Ho Well, uh, I got caught last month. And I just paid the fine. I won't get caught speeding again, that's for sure!

Celia So you see, those cameras *do* work! They *are* a deterrent.

Jin Ho Yeah, that's true. Anyway, would you mind giving me a ride home later? I can't afford to drive for a while.

Unit 6

Carlos Maybe you should change the position of your bed.

Nicole Why? How would that help?

Carlos Well, I've heard that if you sleep with your head to the north, you won't sleep well.

Nicole Really? Who told you that?

Carlos My aunt. She'd always been a terrible sleeper, but when she changed her bed to face east, she slept fine.

Nicole I can't change the position of my bed. My room has a lot of windows, so I can't put my bed against another wall.

Carlos Maybe *that's* the problem! Some Native Americans believe that bad dreams come in through your windows.

Nicole They do? Well, I can't get rid of my windows!

Carlos No, but you could put a dream catcher in a window. You've seen dream catchers, right? They're made of feathers and string and stuff. I've seen them in stores.

Nicole So have I. Huh. Do you think it would work?

Carlos Well, it might. They're supposed to catch the bad dreams before they reach you. And I think they look cool.

Nicole So do I. OK. I'll get one and try it tonight.

Answer key

Unit 1 1. False 2. True 3. False 4. False 5. True 6. False

Unit 2 1. Tracy's sister 2. has 3. the same 4. would 5. is

Unit 3 1. b 2. a 3. a 4. b 5. a

Unit 4 1. True 2. False 3. False 4. True 5. False

Unit 5 1. don't know about 2. punished 3. $600
4. has already paid 5. work 6. give him a ride

Unit 6 1. a 2. b 3. a 4. b 5. b 6. a

Unit 7

Kayla Water's fine. Nice picture! Where did you get it?

Hector At that thrift store downtown.

Kayla Huh. Never been there. They have nice stuff? I mean, as nice as that picture?

Hector Oh, yeah, but a lot of it needs fixing. This picture had a cracked frame, so I had to get it repaired.

Kayla You get anything else there?

Hector Actually, yeah. See this bookcase? Nice, huh?

Kayla Yeah, nice wood. But that shelf is broken.

Hector Yeah, I know. I'm going to get my brother to fix it for me. And look at this clock – this is my favorite!

Kayla Lovely. But . . . it's not working.

Hector It's not? Shoot. Guess that needs fixing, too.

Kayla Bet the battery needs to be replaced, that's all.

Hector Maybe, but . . .

Kayla Yeah, here. Just take this piece off, and . . . Ow! Broke another nail. Huh . . . I can't get this piece off.

Hector Just leave it, then. I'll take it downtown to get it fixed.

Unit 8

Hal Speaking of older people and seats, I hate it when young people sit in those seats that are supposed to be for senior citizens. It's just really rude.

Mara You mean the seats in the front of the bus? I hate that, too. That's like on my bus – those seats have a sign and everything, but last night, they were full of young people.

Hal And someone might have really needed to sit there.

Mara That reminds me of one night last month – the front seats were all full, and this woman got on. She must have been in her 70s, and she looked really exhausted.

Hal I bet no one offered her a seat.

Mara Well, I did, even though I wasn't sitting in one of the special seats, and I was pretty tired. But I got up and pointed to my seat, and I said, "Why don't you sit here?"

Hal She must have been really grateful.

Mara Well, she thanked me, but as soon as she got the seat, she called this little kid over and gave it to him! I stood there thinking I should have kept the seat for myself.

Unit 9

Omar That's true. As long as I can pay my rent, buy food, and have a bit left over for entertainment, that's all I need. You know, it doesn't sound like his money is making them very happy.

Tracy No, and evidently it's hard on Kate. Maggie was telling me how embarrassed Kate feels when he spends a lot of money.

Omar They must have really different lifestyles, too.

Tracy Exactly. Kate once told me she'd be happy living in a little house in the country. But apparently, her fiancé wants to buy a huge luxury apartment in the city.

Omar Well, they say that money is the number one thing that couples fight about.

Tracy Yeah. I've heard that, too.

Omar By the way, I heard that Maggie had broken up with her boyfriend. Is that true? Weren't they going to get married?

Tracy Oh, yeah! That happened last week. She told me all about it.

Omar Did they fight about money, too?

Tracy No. He didn't like her family, and she couldn't stand his friends. Money was the only thing they didn't fight about!

Unit 10

Steve You know, I dropped out of a writing class in college, and now I regret it. After I graduated, I wanted a job in journalism, but I hadn't taken the right classes.

Nela It's hard to see that far into the future, isn't it?

Steve Yeah. If I'd made better decisions back then, I could have had a really good career as a journalist by now.

Nela Well, don't be too hard on yourself. I have a friend who's an editor for a small weekly paper here, and she would never have gotten her job if she hadn't known someone on the staff. Anyway, you like your job, don't you?

Steve Actually, it's pretty boring. If I'd known it was going to be this dull, I never would have accepted it.

Nela Well, you could always get another job, couldn't you? You know, my friend wants to hire an assistant.

Steve Yeah, she'll probably hire some lucky person with connections, who's in the right place at the right time. . . .

Nela Well, you have connections. You know me, don't you? Would you like me to introduce you to my friend?

Steve I sure would! Thanks, Nela. That'd be great.

Unit 11

Ted That's true. Telecommuting is a great way for people with kids to balance jobs and families.

Paula Yeah, in fact, more and more positions at my company are going to telecommuters. We have a lot of working parents.

Ted Right – and people who have really young kids often work part-time or have flexible hours and things like that. Where I work, some jobs are done by two people – you know, job sharing – so that each person can work part-time.

Don Going back to telecommuting, would you like that, Paula?

Paula Actually, I probably wouldn't. Even though it's flexible and convenient and good for the environment and so forth, I just really like working with people.

Ted Well, these days telecommuters are provided with Internet access, video teleconferencing, messaging, and so on, so . . .

Paula I know, but in spite of all that, I prefer dealing with people face-to-face. So many personal interactions are being replaced by technology – for me, it doesn't feel right.

Don I know. That's why flexibility is so great, isn't it? People can work the way they want to.

Unit 12

Jenn You got accepted? Congratulations!

Hiro Thanks. Yeah, it's a 2-year program, but I've already taken some classes. By this time next year, I'll have graduated.

Jenn Great. So, what'll you be studying? Marketing?

Hiro No. Arts management.

Jenn What exactly is arts management? The reason I ask is I don't know if marketing is really working out for me.

Hiro Well, marketing is part of it, but there's a lot more. This fall, I'll be taking business law and business communications.

Jenn That sounds really interesting. I should check it out.

Hiro Well, what I would do is go and ask about the program – tell them about your marketing courses and job experience.

Jenn You're right. I should do that.

Hiro By the way, speaking of jobs – what'll you be doing this summer? Will you be working at the ticket booth again?

Jenn Well, actually, what I was going to tell you was, I've been promoted. I'll be managing the box office this year.

Hiro Perfect experience for arts management! Good for you.

Answer key

Unit 7 1. False 2. True 3. False 4. False 5. True 6. False

Unit 8 1. front 2. tired 3. to be polite 4. gave it away 5. regretted

Unit 9 1. b 2. a 3. a 4. a 5. b 6. b

Unit 10 1. True 2. True 3. False 4. False 5. True

Unit 11 1. parents 2. telecommuting 3. job sharing 4. isn't 5. good

Unit 12 1. a 2. a 3. b 4. a 5. b 6. b